Growing
Language
&

Growing

Language

& Literacy

grades
6–12

STRATEGIES FOR SECONDARY
MULTILINGUAL LEARNERS

Andrea Honigsfeld

HEINEMANN
Portsmouth, NH

Heinemann

145 Maplewood Avenue, Suite 300

Portsmouth, NH 03801

www.heinemann.com

The author and publisher wish to thank those who have generously given permission to reprint borrowed material:

Used with permission of Wiley, from "Getting newcomer English learners off the sidelines: Strategies for increasing learner engagement while developing language and literacy," *TESOL Journal*, L. Auslander, Volume 001–6, 2022 Edition; Permission conveyed through Copyright Clearance Center, Inc.

"All PBL Teachers Should Do These Things" by L. Ayer, published on March 15, 2019. Used with permission.

"Definition of Flipped Learning" by Aaron Sams, Jon Bergmann, Kristin Daniels, Brian Bennett, Helaine W. Marshall, Ph.D., and Kari M. Arfstrom, Ph.D., 2014. Published by the Flipped Learning Network. Used with permission.

Figure 4–20 Thinking Map Summary Table. Available online: https://www.thinkingmaps.com/. Permission was granted by Geoff Suddreth, Thinking Maps, Inc. Used with permission.

"Genre Groups" from *Core Instructional Routines* by Andrea Honigsfeld and Judy Dodge, 2015. Published by Heinemann. Used with permission.

"The Many Levels of Inquiry" by H. Banchi, and R. Bell. 2008. Published in *Science and Children* 46(2): 26–29.

Figure 2–12 from *7 Steps to a Language-Rich, Interactive Classroom* (p. 13), by J. Seidlitz and B. Perryman. Copyright © 2021 by Seidlitz Education. Reprinted with permission.

Library of Congress Control Number: 2024931883

ISBN: 978-0-325-17081-7

eISBN: 978-0-358-96707-1

Aquisitions editor: Holly Kim Price

Editor: Tobey Antao

Production: Sonja S. Chapman

Cover and interior designs: Vita Lane with Suzanne Heiser

Typesetter: Kim Arney

Cover Illustration: Vita Lane

Cover photo of hand: @hulaop/Adobe Stock

Manufacturing: Jaime Spaulding

Printed in the United States of America on acid-free paper

1 2 3 4 5   VP   28 27 26 25 24   PO 4500887050

This book is dedicated to every educator who encounters multilingual learners and offers them love, care, engagement, and support every day!

As with all my publications, I am also dedicating this book to my immediate family: My husband Howard, and my three boys, Benjamin, Jacob, and Noah, who continue to grow their many languages and literacies!

Contents

CHAPTER ONE

Supporting **STARTING** Level Multilingual Learners

CHAPTER THREE

Supporting **DEVELOPING** Level Multilingual Learners 75

CHAPTER FOUR

Supporting EXPANDING Level Multilingual Learners 113

Acknowledgments

I would like to start by acknowledging the entire Heinemann team for seeing the value and impact of the first *Growing Language and Literacy* volume published in 2019 addressed to K–8 educators. Thank you for embracing my vision for a secondary version of the book to also support educators who primarily work with multilingual learners in secondary grades. I would like to recognize Holly Kim Price, who was the editor on the first volume and signed me on to begin work on this second book.

A most sincere appreciation goes to Tobey Antao, my editor on this volume for sharing her passion for this project, for her most sensitive way of handling a difficult transition, for her insightful reading and commenting on every draft, and for her endless patience during our many Zoom calls. A lot of other members of Heinemann deserve a huge shout out as well for tirelessly working on this project, including Suzanne Heiser, design manager, Tessa Hathaway, digital content creator, Elizabeth Tripp, copy editor, and most of all, Sonja Chapman, senior production editor.

A heartfelt thank you to Alycia Owen for being not only a wonderful collaborator and contributor to all the chapters of this book but also my critical friend, who read every draft of each chapter and shared her expertise with me throughout the manuscript development process.

A big thank you goes to Sherry Liptak, proofreader extraordinaire, who somehow always catches every last typo. If any errors remain, they are entirely my responsibility.

I was deeply moved by the generosity of so many educators who directly or indirectly contributed to this book. I would like to express my deepest appreciation and gratitude to all the educators whose work (and whose students' work and pictures) appear in the book. I was awestruck by the hundreds of examples of student and teacher artifacts and beautiful photographs I received to illustrate the points I am making in this book. The hardest job ever was to narrow it down to the dozens of examples I was able to showcase.

So a huge thank you to (in alphabetical order): Johanna Amaro, Katie Beckett, Andrea Bitner, Alicen Brown, Elizabeth Choi, Kelly Cray, Tami Cutter, Andrea Dell'Olio, Elise White Diaz, Jennifer Edwards, Sarah Elia, Holly Ellis, Joseph Fabiano, Lindsey Fairweather, Frank Fonseca, David Gardner, Ashley Garry, Eli Gomes, Mariel Gómez de la Torre-Cerfontaine, Valentina Gonzalez, Mary Beth Gorman, Yuriko Gray, Laura Griffith, Amanda Haleiko, Justine Hernandez, Tan Huynh, Tracy Jackson,

Adile Jones, Meghan Keyser, Michelle Land, Claudia Leon, Kathy Lobo, Shanna Meyer, Neeley Minton, Alycia Owen, Michelle Preng, Jason Raymond, Jane Russell Valezy, Diana Sanchez, Alice Saville, Holly Sawyer, Loretta Schuellein-McGovern, Victoria Seelinger, Monica Starkweather, Nathan Townsend, Laurie Tucker, Terrence Walters, Dan Weinstein, Karla Wilder, Ashley Wong, and Gina Zlaket.

I would also like to acknowledge many other educators, teachers and administrators who have supported this project through their inspiring work, collaboration, and commitment to multilingual learners: Shurook Abdeljaber, Jill Ayabei, Lisa Ball, Danielle Beza, Ellen Brasse, Katelyn Bucchio, Leigh Carter-Fiumara, Evelyn Daza, Kelly DeWitt, Fanny Diaz, Sasha Engelsman, James Fetcho, Emily Francis, Dena Giacobbe, Jo Hawke, Rachel Howell, Joel Johnson, Colleen Jones, Dena Laupheimer, Laurie Lauria, Ashley Lokhandwala, Moira Lust, Shelby Mangan, Nikki McDougal, Irina McGrath, Hayley Naylor, Hannah Oesch, Amy Proctor, Sarah Proctor, Nirmala Ramsaran, Adeline Scibelli, Holly Siggins, and Heather Stumpf.

Last but not least, my sincere gratitude goes to you, the reader of the book! Thank you for joining me in celebrating what our multilingual learners and their teachers can do through the pages of this book!

If you are reading this book, you are likely to be a secondary school educator teaching multilingual learners (MLs), also referred to as English learners (ELs) in many other contexts and publications. Or you might be a student in a teacher education program, just beginning to explore the complexities of the profession, who is eagerly (or perhaps a bit nervously) anticipating what it might be like to work with students who do not speak English (yet!). Or perhaps you are a coach, school or district administrator, or teacher educator who is looking to address the diverse language and literacy proficiencies that coexist in many classrooms. You might have even come across my 2019 book, also called *Growing Language and Literacy*, designed for grades K–8.

> You don't really see the world if you only look through your own window.
>
> —UKRAINIAN PROVERB

If you are reading this book, you are likely already familiar with many of the challenges and joys of guiding these students on a journey of cultural, linguistic, and academic explorations. You know that these students are expected to meet rigorous grade-level standards that might be significantly different from prior learning experiences they had in their home countries. You know that they have to master a large amount of advanced academic, language, and literacy skills in an accelerated fashion to make more than a year's progress each year and catch up to their English-proficient peers to graduate on time. At the same time, you also know that each of your students brings rich life experiences and complex cultural and linguistic identities that add so much to the tapestry of your classroom!

Most importantly, if you are reading this book, you are looking for ways to help your multilingual students flourish academically and socially, no matter where they are on their journey of language development.

I have designed this book to help you in this work. It's a practical book—a ready-to-use, accessible, richly illustrated guide that offers lots of evidence-based and research-informed advice and concrete examples of what works with adolescent multilingual learners. At the same time, it's more than a practical book. The suggestions in these pages offer ways to meet students where they are and to ensure that they can bring their whole selves to school each day. The goal is to help students become successful in our U.S. schools and in society but never at the expense of sacrificing their existing cultural and linguistic competencies.

Language Acquisition 101

Language acquisition (a natural process that happens without much formal instruction) and language learning (intentional learning in the academic context) are strictly separated by some researchers and practitioners. I believe that these processes cannot be artificially separated; thus I will refer to them by the common term *language development*. When I use the term *language proficiency*, I am referring to the child's linguistic competence to process and interpret language (such as listen and read, often coupled with access to visual input as well) and to produce or use expressive language (such as speak and write, frequently accompanied by visual representations). It is critical to recognize the variations that may occur among students and across language domains. Effective instruction will incorporate students' strengths as well as instructional strategies that support students' knowledge of the language and account for their levels of proficiency. Yet a word of caution is in order.

Language development is neither static nor linear. Although there are five consecutive chapters here depicting language progression, offering snapshots of students at various stages of language proficiency, keep in mind that language acquisition is fluid and dynamic. Students come with vast individual differences in their backgrounds and experiences, so at any given moment, some students may exhibit some abilities at a higher proficiency level and other students at a lower one. Language proficiency levels cannot define who a student is; instead, each level simply offers a frame of reference for what the student is able to do (WIDA 2020).

To avoid a static notion of student abilities, maintain a flexible and growth-oriented mindset when working with multilingual learners and when reading this book. Use strategies from across multiple chapters to respond to your students' dynamic language development needs (Heritage, Linquanti, and Walqui 2015) and what, among others, Margo Gottlieb (2021) refers to as *dynamic bilingualism*, the process in which multilingual speakers engage in multiple language interactions using their rich linguistic repertoires.

Focusing on what students can do, as opposed to what they cannot do, is much more likely to make students feel empowered and able to learn English. Too often, discussions of MLs are framed by a deficit model that insists students are at an academic disadvantage because of their cultural, social, and linguistic backgrounds, including their lack of or limited ability to communicate in English. In contrast, an assets-based model of education considers and intentionally builds upon the values, lived experiences, language patterns, and background knowledge students bring and sees them as strengths and advantages that support, not hinder, learning. I agree with de Jong, Yilmaz, and Marichal (2019), who claim,

> It is neither ethical, effective, nor possible or desirable to ask students or teachers to leave their multilingual realities at the school door. In order to support multilingual students' learning and engagement in school, educators must recognize and build on what students already know and our understandings of multilingual development and learning as they develop and implement their curriculum. (109)

In this book I, too, unapologetically advocate for a strengths-based approach to serving MLs in all grade levels, on all proficiency levels, and across all content areas.

Seven Basic Tenets

This book is built on seven tenets that both informed the writing of this book and offer an overarching framework for my work with multilingual learners and their teachers (see Figure I–1 on page xviii).

1. Assets-Based Philosophy

We must recognize multilingual learners and their rich cultural and linguistic backgrounds as social and educational resources for everyone in a school community. Instead of looking at MLs as deficient and lacking knowledge and skills, I take a strengths-based approach to understanding what each student is able to do and how to support them all to reach their full potential. With an assets-based philosophy, you build on students' experiences and deeply connect instruction to students' and their families' lives. In this book, what students can do will be treated as exactly what the students are supposed to do. We cannot remediate what has not been built yet!

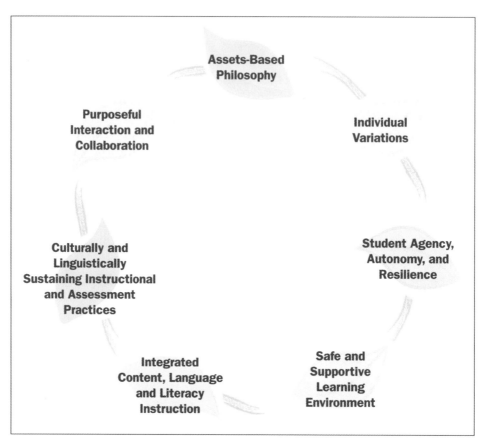

Figure I–1 Seven Core Tenets of Working with Secondary MLs

2. Individual Variations

As a group, multilingual learners represent tremendous diversity, not only culturally, linguistically, and socioeconomically but also based on how much prior knowledge and what type of academic, linguistic, and literacy skills they bring with them when they enter your classroom. Although language proficiency tests are commonly administered in each state to establish incoming students' proficiency levels, it is important to understand that students' trajectory and direction of development may be different in each of the four language domains. In speaking and listening, they may represent one level, and in reading and writing, a quite different one.

Although there are common patterns and predictable stages of language acquisition, MLs are unique individuals who move along the continuum of language learning at different rates. When you work with MLs, you notice that the progress students make week to week, or month to month, or year to year, varies. In addition, MLs may appear to have skills associated with more than one language or literacy development stage; for example, a student may be more advanced in speaking than in writing.

3. Student Agency, Autonomy, and Resilience

Multilingual adolescents must have every opportunity to develop into young adults who fully embrace their personal and educational agency, autonomy, and resilience. CASEL (2021) reminds us that, as educators, we have to expand our pedagogical knowledge and skills to include social-emotional growth. In our planning and lesson delivery for MLs, we must be intentional with SEL (social-emotional learning) so our students "develop healthy identities, manage emotions and achieve personal and collective goals, feel and show empathy for others, establish and maintain supportive relationships, and make responsible and caring decisions" (CASEL 2021). When we support our adolescent multilingual students' agency, autonomy, and resistance, we support them in

> → *using their agency* to define both short-term and long-term academic, linguistic, and personal goals and to pursue those goals purposefully and successfully;
>
> → *using their autonomy* to develop independence and respond to challenges and opportunities—be they academic, linguistic, or personal—by applying their gifts, talents, knowledge, and skills in new contexts; and
>
> → *using their resilience* to learn to manage adverse academic, social, linguistic, and personal experiences and to develop coping mechanisms for facing obstacles in and outside the classroom.

4. Safe and Supportive Learning Environment

All students need a healthy and safe learning environment with trusting relationships in the classroom, in school, and in our larger communities not only to survive and manage but to thrive. This is especially true for multilingual adolescent learners. In the wake of the COVID-19 pandemic, my colleagues and I wrote about the importance of creating "compassionate, engaging learning spaces where collective healing and perseverance shape our pedagogy while we pursue academic excellence and equity for all students" (Honigsfeld et al. 2022, 58). When we intentionally create such a supportive learning environment for MLs by embracing their multilingualism and by creating warm, welcoming physical spaces, they can feel affirmed, seen, and heard. They can take more risks as language learners and develop a stronger sense of belonging.

5. Integrated Content, Language, and Literacy Instruction

Language and literacy learning for multilingual learners does not exist in isolation from the academic curriculum (WIDA 2020). Academic language is recognized as the language used in schools to acquire new or deeper understanding of the core curriculum and to communicate that understanding to others (Gottlieb and Ernst-Slavit 2014). Sarah Ottow (2023) argues for teachers to "think about and operationalize the academic language of our content through which to plan, teach and assess" (17). She refers to this as "developing a language lens," emphasizing that not only will this lens "help us predict what challenges students may have, [but] it can also aid us in discovering opportunities to provide appropriate support and knowledge to plan explicit language goals" (18). With these notions in mind, here I take an approach to introducing strategies that may be used across grade levels and across content areas in support of developing academic language and literacy skills. Mark Pacheco, Shannon Daniel, and Lisa Pray (2017) suggest that "language and content are not separate, and as students engage with different disciplines, they learn to use language practices valued in that discipline" (75). We must see language as a path to equity and an integral part of whatever content we teach (Nordmeyer et al. 2021).

6. Culturally and Linguistically Sustaining Instructional and Assessment Practices

In a seminal essay, Django Paris (2012) carefully differentiates between culturally responsive (Ladson-Billings 2011) and culturally proficient philosophies and argues that students need culturally and linguistically sustaining instruction and assessment. Among so many other practitioners and scholars, more recently, Carla España and Luz Yadira Herrera (2020) have reminded us to understand, honor, celebrate, and elevate bilingual students' experiences. Teachers who engage in these practices not only recognize and respond to students' languages, literacies, and cultural practices but also validate them through multimodal and multilingual learning opportunities. "Rather than framing students' uses of [their home languages] as markers of deficiency, teachers can recognize, praise, and investigate student language use to inform classroom meaning-making" (Pacheco et al. 2019, 77).

7. Purposeful Interaction and Collaboration

Language and literacy development as well as content attainment require students to interact not just with the academic content and their teachers but with each other as well (Zwiers 2019a). In the social-constructivist tradition, I recognize that language does not thrive without ample opportunities to participate in meaningful learning activities that require collaboration. Throughout the book, I emphasize the need for peer interaction, peer-supported learning, and authentic language use that organically includes home languages and nonverbal and multimodal representations.

Research-Informed and Evidence-Based Practices

I have carefully collected and organized the strategies that I present in the five chapters to make sure they are current and as widely applicable to the secondary classroom as possible. They are based on the most current research and evidence-based practices reported by leading researchers and professional organizations. Especially influential are the practice guides published by the Institute of Education Sciences (Baker et al. 2014) and the research and practitioner-oriented work published by TESOL International Association and WIDA Consortium (Shafer Willner et al. 2020). I also acknowledge and build upon the vast practitioner knowledge that is represented by the exceptional teacher and student work samples shared in this book.

The Goals of This Book

In this volume, I unpack the five levels of language acquisition one chapter at a time. I emphasize the common characteristics of learners at each stage and present a unique set of strategies to use with students at each level. These levels are based on the widely used TESOL framework, which is similar to WIDA's framework and other existing frameworks used in the United States and internationally:

1. Starting: being exposed to English with limited language production

2. Emerging: demonstrating receptive and emerging productive language skills

3. **Developing:** employing basic oral and written language skills with predictable error patterns

4. **Expanding:** employing more advanced oral and written language skills with fewer errors

5. **Bridging:** approximating native language proficiency

As Malcolm Gladwell (n.d.) insightfully shares in one of his MasterClass lectures, in order to see something from someone else's perspective and to develop empathy for another person's experiences, we need to listen to their stories. With this in mind, each chapter starts with two composite student vignettes that tell stories of MLs from around the world who have settled in the United States and who are attending middle school or high school. They are inspired by the many conversations I've had with teachers over the past few years.

The next major section of each chapter explores the characteristics of MLs on the target language proficiency level, followed by what I refer to as multidimensional instructional practices and strategies that support each level. The recommended strategies are organized into four main strands:

1. **Social–emotional support strategies** take into consideration the adolescent multilingual learners' unique needs as they develop their language and literacy skills, move through phases of acculturation, and grow in their self-confidence as language learners.

2. **Experiential learning strategies** provide options for consistently enriching language, literacy, and academic content learning via multimodality and innovative, out-of-the-box thinking and teaching.

3. **Strategies for supporting students across multiple modes of communication** take into consideration students' need to use their interpretive and expressive language skills and be successful across the language and literacy domains (WIDA 2020):

   - **Visual literacy strategies** encourage students to both process new learning and express themselves visually.

   - **Oracy strategies** include a range of peer-supported, small-group learning opportunities that require authentic academic conversations. It is well established in the field that "there is no controversy about the fundamental importance of English oral language development as part of the larger enterprise of educating ELLs" (Saunders and O'Brien 2006, 14).

- **Literacy strategies** include ways to enhance MLs' literacy development through carefully crafted scaffolds and multiple tools and activities.

4. **Technology integration strategies** provide tools and techniques to meaningfully utilize well-established and emerging technology tools.

See Figure I–2 for a glimpse into how both students and teachers actively contribute to MLs' language and literacy development in these four strands.

Although the chapters are organized by language proficiency level, most strategies and recommendations may be adapted and successfully transferred to other proficiency levels as well or used with students at multiple levels. Each chapter ends with revisiting the opening vignettes and considering what the students featured in the vignettes will be able to do as they move on to the next proficiency level.

Student and Teacher Engagement in the Four Strategy Strands

Social–Emotional Support

- Students develop as self-directed, self-confident independent learners while also building relationships with others.
- Teachers support their students' agency and autonomy and create a safe, yet challenging learning environment.

Experiential Learning

- Students engage through authentic multimodal learning.
- Teachers infuse multimodality into their teaching through real-life connections.

Figure I–2 *(continues)*

Support Across Multiple Modes of Communication

- *Supporting Visual Literacy*
  - » Students express their thoughts via visuals.
  - » Teachers scaffold student learning with visuals.
- *Building Oracy*
  - » Students participate in a range of authentic academic conversations.
  - » Teachers intentionally connect oracy to literacy.
- *Building Literacy*
  - » Students benefit from multilevel, multilingual, multisensory reading and writing opportunities with increasing complexity and appropriate scaffolds.
  - » Teachers implement multiple approaches to building student literacy.

Technology Integration

- Students use increasingly complex technology critically.
- Teachers guide student language and literacy learning with appropriate technology and scaffolds.

Figure I–2

Chapter One

Supporting

STARTING

Level Multilingual Learners

Meet *Starting* Level Secondary Multilingual Learners

Meet two students, Amanita and Fayeq, who are at the starting level of their English language acquisition. Although they represent different cultural, linguistic, and academic experiences and they attend different schools at different grade levels, they share at least one common characteristic: they are both just beginning to learn English as a new language. As you read their stories, look for cultural, linguistic, and academic assets they possess and consider how you would build upon them. Notice if you have had students with similar backgrounds and responses to being new to secondary school in your context. Stop and reflect on what you would do to help these students get started with English while fully affirming their rich cultural and linguistic heritages, experiences, and identities. How would you welcome them to your classroom so they could be seen, heard, and valued rather than feel discouraged? How would you introduce new concepts and academic skills in a language yet to be acquired without overwhelming them?

> However tall the mountain is, there is a road to the top of it.
> —AFGHAN PROVERB

Amanita

Amanita is a thoughtful, reserved ninth grader, born in Senegal as the oldest of four children. She was educated primarily in French, the official language of Senegal, and completed her preprimary and elementary levels of education and two years of her lower secondary grades (which was no longer compulsory, but her parents insisted). She especially enjoyed her geography classes and learning about different countries around the world as well as ways to protect the environment. Her family members speak Fula among themselves, but everyone in her extended community tends to be communicative in Wolof, too.

When they first arrived in the United States, they lived in a small one-bedroom rental in Little Senegal in New York City and immediately connected with other Senegalese families in the neighborhood. Amanita was asked to look after her younger sisters and little brother a lot, so she did not have much time to make new friends, but she did not really mind. She preferred to read and listen to music, especially to Taylor Swift and Miley Cyrus.

For many generations, Amanita's ancestors, including her great grandparents, were nomadic people. Amanita's grandparents settled down in Podor, the northernmost town of Senegal, and a generation later, her parents ventured into America to have a better education and an opportunity for a professional future for their children. Amanita's mother has quickly established herself as a sought-after hairdresser while her father has been doing several odd jobs, including driving a taxi, volunteering as an interpreter at the Harlem Hospital, and helping out at the local mosque. Her family takes great pride in their traditions, customs, and religion and often cooks *thieboudienne* ("rice with fish") using an old family recipe to re-create the flavors of their homeland.

Amanita's younger siblings all entered the local elementary school together, so she felt relieved that they were safe and had each other and she no longer had to look over them. She had been yearning for more independence, yet she almost immediately became overwhelmed by the size of her new school, the buzz in the hallways, and the complicated schedule she was expected to follow. Just about everything felt so . . . different. Her guidance counselor sensed the tension in her when they first met and sought out another Senegalese student in her grade to connect with Amanita, and whenever possible, she aligned their schedules. Amanita started receiving stand-alone English as a new language (ENL) classes with other newcomers and was placed in an integrated English language arts class with two teachers. The rest of the school day often felt like a blur to her at first, so much moving around from class to class and teacher to teacher, but the frequent check-ins with her French-speaking science teacher helped her get through the toughest parts of the first few weeks. By the end of October, she began to follow along her math and science classes with a bit more confidence, but social studies continued to remain a daily challenge.

→ STOP AND REFLECT ←

What were Amanita's greatest assets as a newcomer to the United States? What could you attribute her progress to? What would you do to further support her acclimation to her new environment and raise her confidence and success in all her courses?

Fayeq

Fayeq is a seventeen-year-old young man from Afghanistan whose family suffered greatly for decades through political and economic hardships. Some of his extended family members are unaccounted for, but most of the family fled to Turkey, seeking asylum or what the Turkish government calls "conditional refugee" status, designed for those needing international protection. Along with his father, mother, and two siblings, Fayeq was evacuated to the United States in the summer of 2021 under the Operation Allies Welcome program and got resettled in Virginia. The family needed a lot of support and guidance in understanding their rights, getting food and housing, accessing health services, enrolling the children in school, and exploring job opportunities for the adults.

Although Fayeq did quite well in school in Herat, his life had been in turmoil for some time, and he had not been able to focus on his education for several weeks before leaving Afghanistan in a hurry. Facebook was his main source of reading and accessing news about his homeland and some friends who were still there.

Fayeq's father has often reminded him to live up to his name, which means "outstanding" or "distinguished," and said that he has great hopes and high expectations for his only son. Fayeq's counselor explained to his parents that since he entered the U.S. school system in Virginia in eleventh grade, he had a reduced credit requirement to graduate, and the local school district's newcomer center would be the best place for him to start out. The center is specially designed to welcome secondary students like him and support them with the vast educational and cultural adjustments they need to make when they first arrive in the United States.

When Fayeq began his new school year in mid-September with minimal delay, he felt that things might start calming down a bit around him. But he misses riding his bike around the Old City of Herat. He understands some everyday English and can maintain a brief conversation with classmates and teachers, but he most appreciates having access to sports activities during and after his school day. His soccer coach has been looking out for him from day one, but it is even more important to him that his teammates have taken him right in, which has eased his frustration with school. He knows he will need to work hard to reach his goals: he is determined to graduate from high school with a standard diploma and seek further education in engineering.

> → **STOP AND REFLECT** ←
> Why is it important to understand the complex experiences that Fayeq brings to school? In what ways should Fayeq's teachers respond to the trauma that he has lived through? What assets can his teachers tap into? What would you do to help him thrive in the newcomer center and beyond?

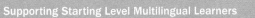

Look Beyond the Label

As the label suggests, starting level students are uniquely positioned to begin a new journey, which is likely to be both exhilarating and—at times—exhausting for students and teachers alike! When starting level secondary students enter the U.S. school system and are assessed for language proficiency, they may produce minimal, formulaic language ("Thank you," "Hello") in English or nothing at all, and they may not recognize what is being spoken or read to them. They may be able to identify many written words that are internationally known and frequently appear as part of the environmental print (for example, a stop sign; some brand names with logos, such as Coca-Cola, Nike, and Microsoft; and names of common tech tools or apps, like iPad, Instagram, and Twitter). These students have vast life and language experiences connected to their birth countries and home cultures, so welcoming them as resources and valued members in their new school and classroom community is vital for them not only to survive but to thrive.

Let's also recognize that starting level students come with a wide range of educational background experiences; they may be "at all different ages and with many unique needs, including having experienced gaps in formal schooling (SLIFE students), having fled dangerous situations (refugees and others), having disabilities, and being in the U.S. without parents (unaccompanied minors)" (Umansky et al. 2018, 24). Some might carry years of trauma and unimaginable tragedies; others might have arrived as academically accomplished teenagers having had a variety of advanced learning opportunities as well as high levels of understanding and skills in some core content areas such as math and science. Many are already bilingual, biliterate, or bidialectal, while some might even be multilingual. They all bring their hopes and dreams, fears and inhibitions, unique talents and interests, spirit, and resiliency with them. While researching how to facilitate meaning making for refugee-background youth (RBY), Carrie Symons and Yue Bian (2022) remind us of the need for "researchers, practitioners, and community organizations to work together to design educational experiences and environments that are affirming and responsive to RBY's unique assets, forms of knowledge, approaches to meaning-making, and learning needs" (2). I would argue that same urgency applies to welcoming all newcomers.

Since many starting level students—though not all of them—are recent arrivals, they are likely to benefit from consistent, predictable routines and structures in your classroom. With careful scaffolding, ample visual support, and attention to creating a context for learning and building background knowledge (that either they possess or you purposefully build about everyday topics or academic content), they can gain an overall understanding of what you present in your class. They begin to use words, phrases, and short sentences that they may have memorized as a chunk of language (e.g., "Can you help me, please?" "Can I use the bathroom?") with increasing confidence. They are just starting to develop foundational language and literacy skills in English, hence the name *starting.*

Elizabeth Choi and her colleagues welcome newcomers in their middle school with a friendly document using lots of home language support. See Figure 1–1 for the cover page of their welcome kit, which includes words in Spanish, Korean, and Japanese while also teaching some necessary English words.

Some students may start out on the same level for the four key language domains, namely listening, speaking, reading, and writing; others may have some receptive—also referred to as interpretive—skills gained through some prior experience with English or familiarity with popular songs, movies, or video games. Yet others might have had limited or no prior exposure to either formal or informal English. Soon enough, you can observe that most newcomers are beginning to understand and process what is happening around them and what is being spoken or read to them. Make sure you not only attend to all four language domains but add visual access points and invite visual representations. Notice how their interpretive skills (especially listening) tend to develop more rapidly than the productive—also referred to as expressive—language skills (speaking and writing). The trajectory of certain literacy skills is also predictable: figuring out the English alphabet if their home language uses a different orthography may come earlier than developing reading comprehension skills, yet rich visual support will help them understand the gist of your lessons. Similarly, you should expect students to use shorter verbal expressions and visual note-taking and multimodal, multilingual communication before they write in English with cohesion or fluency.

Many of your starting level secondary students will demonstrate accelerated growth and relatively fast advancement to the next level, called emerging (see Chapter 2), whereas others will need additional time to show the progress they are making because of multiple interconnected academic, linguistic, cultural, and social-emotional reasons. Keep the following mantra in mind: "*lower is faster, higher is slower*" (Sahakyan 2013, 2). This research-informed principle suggests that multilingual learners in lower grades and those who are at lower proficiency levels (starting and emerging, and even developing) tend to acquire language at faster rates, whereas those in higher grades or at higher proficiency levels (such as developing and expanding levels or above) will experience a slower rate of growth. Patience and perseverance—yours and theirs—are much-needed resources.

As you can see in Figure 1–2, the starting level of language proficiency has many other labels, depending on the theoretical framework you refer to, the state or country you live in, or the language development standards you use. Keep in mind that the descriptions for each category by the various professional organizations will be rather similar but might not completely overlap.

Welcome to Farragut Middle School!

This paper contains important information that will help you be successful.

Este documento contiene información importante que le ayudará a tener éxito.

이 백서에는 성공하는 데 도움이 되는 중요한 정보가 포함되어 있습니다.

このペーパーには、成功に役立つ重要な情報が含まれています。

Your Grade	Your Pod	Homeroom Teacher: Room:
Student Number (ID)		Chromebook Username: Password:
Lunch Time	Lunch Code	Bus Number: AM Pick-up: PM Pick-up:

Helpful Phrases in English	
Good morning Buenos días 좋은 아침 おはよう	I don't understand. No entiendo. 모르겠어요 理解できない
Please show me. Por favor, muéstrame 보여주세요 を見せて下さい	I need help. Necesito ayuda. 도움이 필요해 私は助けが必要です
Thank you Gracias 고맙습니다 ありがとうございました	May I use the restroom? ¿Puedo usar el baño? 화장실 사용해도 되겠습니까? お手洗いを使ってもいいですか？

Figure 1–1   Welcome Kit

Other Labels for Starting Level		
TESOL	**Hill and Miller (2014)**	**WIDA**
Starting	Preproduction	Entering

ELPA (2016)	**New York**	**California**	**Texas**
Emerging	Entering	Emerging	Beginner

Figure 1–2

Consider What the Research Says

The stage of language acquisition referred to as *starting* in this book was first described as *preproduction* by Krashen and Terrell (1983). The preproduction stage (sometimes also referred to as the silent period) may last up to six months, and it is often characterized by—as its name suggests—accumulating receptive language skills but not yet producing any or much language in spoken or written form. Not all starting level students may need several months to advance to the next level, so be prepared for vast individual variances. As beautifully stated by Ohta (2001), the "seemingly silent learner is neither passive nor disengaged but is involved in an intrapersonal interactive process" (12). The heart and mind are never silent! You might wonder what you can do about this. Advancing through the first stage of language development is a complex process, so I invite you to embrace your role as a linguistic and cultural mediator and language facilitator: you can mediate the intrapersonal linguistic process by providing multidimensional modes of communication and learning opportunities while honoring the learners' private speech, including internal thoughts and (*seemingly*) silent participation in learning. Figure 1–3 shows how one newcomer demonstrated his understanding visually. When secondary ELL teacher Andrea Bitner asked her beginners to write down what they knew about ants, they offered a few words. Then one student came up to the whiteboard and produced a complex drawing, revealing his knowledge and understanding of ant colonies.

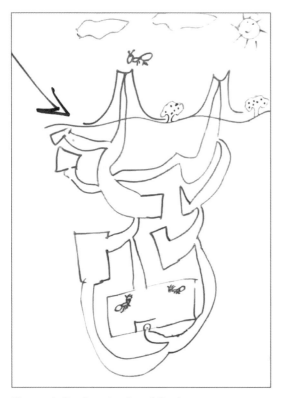

Figure 1–3 Starting Level Student Demonstrating Complex Understanding

Research has also well documented that starting level students' home languages and identities are critical resources. Gholdy Muhammad's (2020) passionate call to educators to fully embrace a historically responsive literacy is also applicable to multilingual starting level students: let's commit to exploring and building on the histories, cultures, identities, literacies, and language practices of students so they can all develop a strong sense of belonging.

An important finding from research on bilingualism is relevant for all MLs, especially for those who do not yet communicate in English. Christensen (2010) suggests that "by bringing students' languages from their homes into the classroom, we validate their culture and their history as topics worthy of study" (33). Other research shows that students authentically engage in multilingual practices for both social and academic purposes and both individually and collaboratively (French 2018).

More recently, Mandy Stewart and her colleagues (2021) researched disciplinary literacy and multilingualism in the high school context and concluded that "in place of official bilingual education programs that cannot account for all languages in a diverse environment, a more practical approach might be to apply a translingual literacy lens" (182), which includes understanding how multilingualism works and opening a learning space up to multilingual engagement. The best part: you don't have to be multilingual as an educator to do this (although you might find it affirming and exciting to dabble in multiple languages and let your students teach you some important phrases).

An important research-informed practice is to create a supportive environment for all students by valuing not just bilingualism in an individual person but plurilingualism in the community (Dover and Rodríguez-Valls 2022). My call to action to you is to make all students' linguistic heritages and language practices visible and valued. When students' home languages are used and affirmed in school, their emergent bilingual and bicultural identities are also affirmed, and the bridge to learning English is established. Among many others, Fred Genesee (2023), Valentina Gonzalez (2022), and Elsa Billings and Aída Walqui (2021) firmly advocate for recognizing multilingual learners' home languages as valuable resources. I invite you to support English acquisition through your students' home language use by exploring connections (including cognates and other similarities) between students' home languages and English; comparing how certain grammatical structures work in English versus in the home language (e.g., Spanish places the adjectives after, not before, the nouns), thus raising metalinguistic awareness; letting students choose whether to complete some tasks such as a prewriting activity in English or in the home language; and creating bilingual peer bridges for in-class discussions.

Most recently, Kristen McInerney (2023), professor of curriculum and pedagogy at George Washington University, has reported that through home language use during peer-to-peer interaction, newcomers "explained, clarified confusion, took the initiative of helping others, called and texted peers to get them into virtual classes, and made friends while helping each other out" (22); thus they began to participate in academic and social encounters while building a sense of community.

Understand Starting Level Learners

Most starting level secondary students are newcomers to the United States. Many students have grown up in complex cultural and linguistic contexts provided by their parents and extended family members. They might have had exposure to some U.S. cultural and linguistic experiences through social media or pop culture. With this in mind, let's look at what positive expectations you can have for starting level students or, as aptly put by WIDA (2020), what these students *can do*. These accomplishments are not expected on the very first day or even in the first weeks; some will develop over the course of many days, weeks, or even months. Also keep in mind that the actual list of what students can do is much longer and much more elaborate than any book could capture, so enjoy this journey of exploration with your starting level students.

When it comes to *listening*, you can expect students to begin to show evidence of comprehending English by doing the following:

→ responding with gestures rather than words (nodding, shaking their heads, making hand gestures)

→ responding nonverbally to simple, frequently used classroom commands ("Come here!")

- → identifying classmates and teachers by their names
- → becoming familiar with the sounds and rhythms of the English language
- → recognize everyday classroom language (words and short phrases) associated with daily routines, and directions given by teachers (*open your books, agenda, do now, exit slip, homework*)
- → recognizing and responding to formulaic language ("Hello," "Thank you," "How are you?")

Regarding *speaking* skills, you will notice that students initially respond and communicate nonverbally by nodding, gesturing, or choosing to communicate in their home language. They will incrementally expand their English-speaking skills by doing the following:

- → offering one-word answers such as "Yes" and "No"
- → code switching or translanguaging (using their home language intertwined with some English words) for communication in response to English prompts (see more discussion of translanguaging in Chapter 2)
- → repeating words and phrases commonly used by others in familiar settings ("I forgot my homework")
- → calling their teachers and classmates by name
- → using formulaic language ("I don't understand," "Can you help me, please?")

In Jennifer Edwards' classes, students regularly interact with each other to make sense of visually presented material (see Figure 1–4).

When it comes to *reading*, some students are likely to be nonreaders in English, whereas others will readily build on and transfer their literacy skills from their home languages. At this stage, I would anticipate them to develop some foundational skills such as the following:

- → reading environmental print (exit sign, classroom labels, anchor chart headings)
- → relying on visual literacy skills or visual support for understanding what others read aloud or present verbally to them

Figure 1–4 Students Make Sense of a Graph Together

→ recognizing the letters of the English alphabet (when coming from a different writing system)

→ making letter-sound connections

→ recognizing high-frequency words

→ enjoying visually rich presentations that are well supported with other nonverbal cues

→ using bilingual dictionaries to look up words

Finally, in the area of *writing*, students may begin to do the following:

→ form letters of the English alphabet (when coming from a different writing system)

→ print frequently used words including their names or headings for student work

→ copy words or longer texts

→ draw sketches or diagrams using their home language and literacy skills

→ create illustrations or other graphic representations of their ideas with word labels in English or both of their languages

→ write in their home language and add labels or key words in English

Consider your expectations for starting level students. Secondary students are resourceful, which is a really good thing: they need to use all the resources available in their home languages, accessible through their in-school and out-of-school support systems, and manageable through the power of their own resilience and determination. They also need meaningful exposure to English to begin to comprehend and respond to what you're presenting or exploring in your classroom. They are most likely to succeed and progress when support is given in *multiple* ways, in *multiple* languages, and through *multiple* modalities. For example, I would engage Amanita from the beginning of the chapter in all the languages available to her. She will build English language skills through accessing her prior knowledge, engaging in teacher-guided and peer-supported short yet rigorous explorations, and participating in purposeful small- and large-group discussions that may include French and English language use. She can use simple sentences to explain what she has read with the help of sentence starters and patterned language. She can also count on getting emotional support from other Senegalese students through an after-school culture club. To support Fayeq, I would create a range of meaningful, interactive, visually supported learning opportunities as well as ways for him to express his ideas through sketching. Although he might not be able to use English at the eleventh-grade level, I would challenge him cognitively and give him every chance to think at grade level as he encountered complex content through visuals, digital media, multilingual resources, and peer interactions.

Begin Here with Starting Level Students

Starting level students will be best supported through teaching techniques that are multidimensional linguistically, culturally, and academically. For example, students will access learning activities that allow them to be fully engaged by listening to others (both teachers and peers) discuss something they can start to figure out, make sense of, and relate to. They can also watch and listen to digital recordings that are carefully *created* (you make it) or *curated* (you find it) to make sure the students can access them and simultaneously process the visual and verbal inputs (see more on technology integration later in the chapter). When it comes to contributing to class, multidimensionality means that you find ways for students to participate without being pressured to use English, such as expressing themselves in their home language or another language they are communicative in by working with language partners, nonverbally using TPR (total physical response), visually, artistically, or through movement. If they are literate in a language other than English, encouraging students to use that language is critical for academic, cultural, social-emotional, and linguistic development.

When you have students at the starting level in your class, make sure that they feel welcome and included in the classroom and school community. Three practices to implement are (1) establishing a support system, (2) using what is familiar to your new students as a primary source of—and essential link to—learning, and (3) building basic comprehension and communicative language in English.

Establish a Support System

When you have a new student in your class, regardless of the age or background, that student is likely to face some challenges as they begin to adjust to the new school and classroom environment, accept the changes in routines, understand the social and academic expectations, adhere to the written and unwritten rules of being a student, make new friends, and build trust in relationships with both peers and adults. When your new student is a multilingual learner, the situation may be exacerbated by cultural and linguistic differences, so an important first step is to help the student develop a sense of belonging by creating a safe and welcoming environment.

Based on her research with secondary-age newcomers, Lisa Auslander (2022) reported that "students described collaboration as one of their lifelines, because it allowed them to be part of a larger community of learners, to feel a sense of belonging, and to encourage a willingness to take risks" (4). Students can build relationships one classmate at a time in a more systematic way if you assign various roles to a number of peers in your classroom:

> → A *language partner* will do just what the name suggests: use all of the available languages and linguistic resources such as code switching and translanguaging to communicate essential information.
>
> → A *literacy partner* will read with the classmate and share their writing with the multilingual student while also offering encouragement for home language use.
>
> → A *study partner* will review and practice in-class and homework assignments.
>
> → A *writing partner* will discuss the prompt, brainstorm ideas, draft through translanguaging, sketchnote together, write collaboratively, offer peer feedback to early drafts, and help with revising and editing.

Experienced international educator Alycia Owen suggests that you set up peer-led school tours that include introductions to key personnel such as the guidance counselor, principal, nurse, librarian, and coaches as well as peer support for using a printed schedule showing class rotations and navigating special events like assemblies and extracurricular activities such as clubs and sports. High school ELL teacher Yuriko Gray helps her newcomers acclimate to school while also building community through role-playing (see Figure 1–5).

It is helpful if the partner system includes students who speak the same language as your newcomer, but it may not be possible in many classrooms. It is always a good idea to ask students to volunteer to be a buddy and to select ones who are known to be patient, empathetic, and more than willing to take risks and learn from their peers. Also, remember to regularly check in with the partners and change them up so more students have the opportunity to help. Based on the class dynamics, you may want to create a system that includes all your students or rotate the partners to expand the opportunities for positive student-to-student interactions across cultural and linguistic backgrounds. Partnering MLs with others is a strong way to build peer acceptance and leadership skills among the more proficient students in the class while enhancing a positive class culture where everyone can thrive. Just imagine the many ways students can contribute to peer learning experiences. For example, "collaborative posters can be a productive way for students to demonstrate leadership in working with a group, apply artistic skills, discuss ideas in the home language and present ways that ideas connect visually" (Auslander 2022, 3–4).

Capitalize on Familiarity

More than any other group of MLs, starting level students need to feel that they belong and can learn English while their home cultures and languages are also affirmed. Imagine that you are an adolescent. You are trying to figure out who you are in this world and define your identity, but then you move to a place where not too many people understand your inner struggles, know the joys, hopes, and dreams you have grown up with, share the customs and holidays that your family cherishes, or enjoy the food that nourished you. How would you adjust to a new environment?

One powerful way you can welcome newcomers is by making them feel a strong sense of belonging and incorporating resources into your teaching that will be familiar to them. Start by learning to say all your students' names correctly and finding out the meaning or significance of their names. This reminds me of so many literary works (or relevant excerpts from them) you can explore with your students: *The Namesake*, by Jhumpa Lahiri (2003), *My Name Is Jorge: On Both Sides of the River*, by Jane Medina (1999), *Darius the Great Is Not Okay*, by Adib Khorram (2019), *Don't Ask Me Where I Am From*, by Jennifer Leon (2020), just to

Role-Playing Practice Script

ROLES	LINES
New Student	Hi. I am new here.
Student 1	Hello. I can help you. What is your name?
New Student	My name is _____.
Student 2	Excuse me. Please spell your name for me.
New Student	A-B-C-D-E-F-G-H-I-J-K-L-M-N-O-P-Q-R-S-T-U-V-W-X-Y-Z.
Student 1	Thank you. My name is _____. Nice to meet you.
Student 2	My name is _____. Good to meet you.
New Student	I need help. I want to go to class.
Student 3	Do you have a program? It looks like this.
New Student	Yes.
Student 4	Do you want help with your program?
New Student	Yes, please help me.
Students 3 & 4	OK. Show us your program.
New Student	Here is my program.
Student 1	First period is from 8:15 to 9 o'clock.
	Look at my clock and I will show you 8:15.
Student 2	Second period is from 9:03 to 9:48.
	Look at my clock and I will show you 9:03.
Student 3	Third period is from 9:51 to 10:36.
	Look at my clock and I will show you 9:51.
Student 4	Fourth period is from 10:39 to 11:24.
	Look at my clock and I will show you 10:39

Figure 1–5

name a few. Most recently I read *Silk Tether* by Minal Khan (2016), in which she reflects on the importance of one's name:

What's in a name? Everything, I thought. It is a birth-given label, like a barcode on every book that, though we may like it or not, distinguishes us. It gives us security. We are living in a globalized world now, where people take on multiple identities as easily as trying out new outfits. Our name is now the only real, permanent truth to us. (ebook, Chapter 8)

→ Learn some key phrases such as "Welcome," "Glad to see you," and "I am your math [science/social studies/language arts] teacher" in your new student's home language. Better yet, continue to learn phrases from your student by inviting them to be your teacher.

→ Create a word wall that has some welcoming words or content-specific key concepts in every language represented in your classroom.

→ Use images (photos, sketchnotes, diagrams, videos) that your starting level students can recognize when you illustrate key concepts.

→ Integrate starting level students into small-group discussion tasks by using "themes and essential questions to leverage students' prior knowledge and experience" (Auslander 2022, 2).

→ When establishing classroom routines and procedures, incorporate print and visual cues and digital reminders.

→ Teach words and phrases directly related to the class and school environment. Thorpe (2017) also suggests to "use the students' immediate surroundings to expand their vocabulary" (18).

Moll and his colleagues' (1992) seminal work focuses on recognizing that all students come to school with tremendous knowledge derived from home- and community-based shared experiences that are often unrelated to the taught curriculum and skills needed for academic success. Moll calls this *funds of knowledge*. When the knowledge students accumulate at home or through their vast out-of-school experiences is connected to who they are, the term used is *funds of identity*. Esteban-Guitart and Moll

(2014) suggest that "funds of knowledge—bodies of knowledge and skills that are essential for the well-being of an entire household—become funds of identity when people actively use them to define themselves" (31). When we recognize students' funds of knowledge, we encourage them to feel valued by connecting their learning with the cultural knowledge they bring to school. Funds of knowledge and funds of identity are rich "tool kits" (73) created from the students' lived experiences.

When a newcomer enters your classroom, embrace what they know and who they are and consider them as a major source of information as well as a way to bridge to the curriculum, the new culture, and the language they are about to acquire (Helman et al. 2016; Salva 2017; Samway, Pease-Alvarez, and Alvarez 2020). Consider all the ways you can help your MLs see aspects of their out-of-school cultural and linguistic experiences reflected in the school environment and the learning activities. Some of these suggestions impact the larger school community, so your role might be to advocate on behalf of MLs to ensure the school does the following:

→ Place signs around the building welcoming students and families in all the languages spoken in the community.

→ Prepare infographics, information booklets, or English Language Development (ELD) handbooks, in all the languages spoken in the community.

→ Make sure school staff feel comfortable greeting and interacting with adults who do not speak English well, using cues and resources that illustrate frequently communicated processes.

→ Make online resources on the school or district website and digital media available in languages other than English.

→ Make interpreters available on site or on call as needed to support family meetings.

→ Have student ambassadors who welcome new students into the school community, offer tours of the building, and join the new students at recess and other unstructured times.

→ Let students tell their personal stories, make connections to text—both fiction and nonfiction—and make sense of their way of life at home.

Middle and high school emergent bilingual specialist Michelle Preng works with interpreters to hold learning events for newcomer families. Students and

Figure 1–6   Family Members Learning Together

caregivers learn how to access and utilize the school's learning management system and how to help support their students from home (see Figure 1–6).

Newcomers benefit from a positive welcoming experience within the first few weeks of their arrival, including individual meetings with a designated guidance counselor and family liaison and attending a new student orientation for students and their caregivers. A newcomer kit or welcome kit may also be a helpful resource with some key information (Colorín Colorado n.d.). A kit might include guidance regarding

→ how to navigate the school: a colorful map that shows where to find some key places (bathrooms, nurse's room, cafeteria)

→ how to find the various classrooms: classroom location and teacher's name and phone number or email

→ routines regarding arrival and dismissal—especially if busing is involved and MLs need to find their way to the correct school bus

→ routines and expectations about lunch time

→ a list of key community-based organizations and resources such as names and numbers of other families who have volunteered to offer help

→ a basic English dictionary of key words, phrases, and sentences translated into the student's home language

→ information for parents in languages they understand

See Figure 1–7 for an excerpt from the newcomer welcome packet that Pam Schwallier, director of EL and bilingual programs at West Ottawa Public Schools, created.

Welcome to *West Ottawa* High School!

Hi!

My name is _____.

I speak _____.

I'm from _____.

I'm in _____ grade.

IMPORTANT INFORMATION

My Schedule

	Time & room number	Subject & teacher
1st hour		
2nd hour		
Power		
3rd hour		
4th hour		
Lunch		
5th hour		
6th hour		

My Bus	My Locker	My Student Number
Bus Number	Locker number: Locker Combination: Left: ← Right: → Left: ←	

My computer login	People to know:
User Name: Password:	Principal: Counselor: ESL Teacher:

Figure 1–7 Introductory Pages from a Secondary Newcomer Welcome Packet

Build Basic Comprehension and Communication Skills

At the very onset of language acquisition, your starting level MLs will want to understand what is happening around them and learn how to communicate their needs. How can you help them develop language skills to respond to their immediate needs?

→ Attach language to objects and actions. Allowing beginner MLs to hear the words that are connected to objects and actions commonly used in the classroom will help develop basic vocabulary.

→ Create a weekly schedule or an agenda for each class that is visually supported with diagrams or images. Not only will your MLs develop familiarity with the structure of your lessons and understand what your expectations are, but they will also learn—first to recognize and then to articulate—some key words and phrases.

$\rightarrow$ Use as many different kinds of in-class support as possible, such as shared-language partners, colleagues, and volunteers as well as technology-enhanced supports. Turn on closed captioning in English when you show a video, encourage electronic print and dictionary use, and make sure iPads and other tablets are supplied with apps that help translate words and phrases (rather than whole sentences or longer passages) with accuracy.

Focus on Multidimensional Strategies

Here I present a selection of multidimensional instructional practices and strategies for supporting starting level students. I have organized the recommended strategies into four main strands: (1) social-emotional support; (2) experiential learning support; (3) support across multiple modes of communication (including supporting visual literacy, building oracy, and building literacy); and (4) technology integration. As you will notice, this organization will recur in each subsequent chapter to target the rest of the proficiency levels as well. The strategies that are woven throughout the book will offer some foundational skills for starting level students. An important word of caution: you can use many of these strategies with all levels of language proficiency, so as you read through the book, try to avoid limiting your strategy use to the designated language proficiency level where the strategy is first introduced.

Social–Emotional Support for Adolescent MLs

When you welcome new MLs, put yourself in their shoes and consider—through the eyes of each person—what their first impressions might be. What do they see and hear? What do they notice and wonder about? Keep in mind that if they don't understand your verbal input, they will certainly be more responsive to nonverbal cues they can "read": your body language, facial impressions, smiles and frowns, gestures, tone of voice, and so on.

Let's flip the coin: What are *your* first impressions of your newcomers? What do you first notice about your secondary MLs at the starting level? How about their peers—what do they see when a newcomer walks through the doors of your classroom? Tung's (2013) caution to us is as apt now as it was a decade ago: let's not view multilingual "education as a problem, dilemma, achievement gap, or crisis"; instead, she urges us to "embrace ELLs as the very community members who, when well educated, will be the bicultural, bilingual leaders who improve our city neighborhoods and help us participate effectively in the global economy" (4).

As newcomers, they need to orient themselves to so many new things! To thrive, they need to develop self-confidence in a new school, neighborhood, state, or country. And let's not forget: they have to do all this in a new language! It is expected that many of your newcomers will experience some level of anxiety and fear, especially if their mental, physical, and social needs are shaped by dislocation and trauma and their academic self-concepts are shaped by limited or interrupted prior education.

What can we all agree to do?

- First and foremost, let's create a safe, welcoming learning environment.
- Let's make sure MLs feel seen, heard, and valued in the school community.
- Let's acknowledge the many challenges newcomers and their families must face daily as they process leaving everything familiar or, in the case of refugees, leaving highly disturbing situations behind.
- Let's celebrate MLs for their courage, perseverance, and commitment to working hard every day to adjust to the norms and characteristics of a new country, community, and school setting.
- Let's intentionally give MLs ample opportunities to engage in explorations of their identities, to create positive self-definitions, and to develop an affirming vision for their future.

It's impossible to overstate the importance of relationships. Kristen McInerney's (2023) study on the predictors and experiences newcomer multilingual adolescents have in a high school further validates it. She found that the close to five hundred students they surveyed utilized "an intricate web of support from peers, staff, and families that contributed to their sense of belonging so that school felt like a second family or second home" (22). They also appreciate learning from classmates who come from other cultures and speak other languages as they establish common interests and common languages (English or another lingua franca with them).

Kelly Cray, a cultural and language support teacher, not only creates a welcoming, homelike learning environment but also ensures that her starting level students can interact with same-language peers to accomplish complex academic tasks (see Figure 1–8).

Experiential Learning Support

Figure 1–8 Student Interactions Are Best When You Encourage Them to Use Multiple Languages

Based on Vygotsky's theory of the zone of proximal development, Catherine R. Rhodes and colleagues (2021) suggest that from adolescence on, we can "think fully in concepts, engaging in abstraction without having to ground concepts in the empirical" (525). While the adolescent brain undergoes rapid maturation when it comes to concept formation and the emergence of an expanding worldview, starting level MLs, especially those who remain in the preproduction stage and do not respond verbally yet, are most productive and participatory in classroom activities when they can show their understanding and develop new knowledge and skills without much verbal output in the new language. You will significantly enhance content learning and language acquisition for newcomer MLs if you include hands-on explorations.

I realize that there's often a perception that manipulatives and games are just for younger kids. However, when we think about the ways in which historical artifacts in museums spark understanding; the ways in which hands-on experience hones skills; and the ways in which simulations train professionals in fields such as aviation and health care, it's clear that purposeful use of manipulatives and games can boost students' comprehension and skills.

When we intentionally attach language to action and objects, it helps MLs make connections between English words and phrases and the concepts, qualities, or actions they represent. Add real objects or manipulatives to lessons that require describing, sequencing, measuring, comparing, contrasting, inferring, and a range of other skills that students must develop. It will come more naturally and easily in some content areas than others. For example, when you introduce the safety rules and safety equipment in your science lab, verbally label the various tools such as the first aid kit, safety goggles, and protective gloves as you demonstrate their use and allow the students to handle them, too. These school resources may be new to some of your newcomer students, so allow time for them to become comfortable with navigating these new experiences.

While visual support is powerful (see the next section, which focuses on just that), no photo or video can replace the real objects, also referred to as *realia* in the context of language pedagogy. This "object-based learning" (Baldioli 2022), as it's known in museum education, integrates opportunities for close observation, critical reflection, and deep thinking. Your starting level MLs (and your other students) will love them.

So whenever possible, use realia. If realia is not available, try some models or manipulatives that are either commercially made or produced by teachers and students. Joseph Fabiano collects World War I realia to supplement instruction in his tenth-grade global history class. In Figure 1–9, he holds a 1915 World War I airplane, a piece of trench art made by a French soldier along the Western Front. The plane is made from bullet casings with 1880s French Napoleon III coins as landing gear wheels.

Figure 1–10 offers some other further examples of using realia connected to some frequently taught lessons. As you envision lessons using realia, plan to name the objects for students and to allow the students to handle them and experience them physically.

When we reduce the anxiety about being in a new environment and learning a new language, starting level MLs may become much more receptive to English. Game-like activities (such as sorting and sequencing images) lower the affective filter (the emotional factors that may impact language acquisition positively or negatively—first discussed by Krashen [1988]) and invite MLs to be more receptive to new experiences with the language. Brain breaks in your secondary classroom can include movement-related activities or mechanical puzzles such as the famous Rubik's Cube or other twisty puzzles (yes, that's their official name). You can make these puzzles available and let students choose to engage with them or not: while the puzzles might help some students relax or feel validated, others might simply find them annoying.

Total physical response is—as I overheard in a recent workshop—a blast from the past. As suggested by the name of this strategy, it incorporates some sort of small or

Figure 1–9   Taking a Closer Look at Artwork Made in the Trenches of World War I in 1915. Photo Credit: Adile Jones Photography

Some Ways to Use Realia in Secondary Classrooms		
Subject Matter	**Lesson Focus**	**Use of Realia**
ELA	Short story/ novel/poetry	• Use music from the era depicted in the literary selections • Select objects that play an important role in the piece • Place one or more objects in a paper bag and have students guess what the object is and what role it will play in the literary selections
Social Studies	American consumerism	• Use print and TV advertisements and actual objects or replicas of them to analyze modern amenities and popular goods for impact on people's lifestyle and choices
Math	Geometry	• Paper plates • Paper folding • Tangrams
Science	Lab experiments	• Lab equipment • Necessary materials for the experiments

Figure 1–10

large motor movement and requires students to respond nonverbally to what the teacher is asking or modeling, such as using a motion or gestures or responding to a command with gestures and actions (such as acting out verbs or adjectives). Variations of the strategy have been used for decades (first mentioned by Asher in [1981]) to enhance beginner language learners' active engagement. If you want to adapt it for your secondary classroom, you have a few choices and opportunities for creative implementation:

→ Have all students respond nonverbally using a thumbs-up for agreeing and thumbs-down for disagreeing with a statement.

→ Have students raise one hand for *yes* and two hands for *no*.

→ Have students wave one hand if they like or agree with something in a class discussion and raise the roof by waiving with two hands if they *really* like something.

→ Have students watch as you use facial expressions or gestures to demonstrate differences between adjectives such as *mad* and *horrified* or verbs such as *walk* and *stroll*. You can invite your students to start acting out those differences when they are ready as you attach language to the movement.

Support Across Multiple Modes of Communication

Starting level adolescent multilingual learners want to communicate. They will not be able to do so fluently in English yet, so you must make a range of modalities and scaffolds available to apprentice them into the academic and linguistic tasks waiting for them. Inviting a variety of types of participation will increase the likelihood they will attempt to communicate in their new language.

Supporting visual literacy

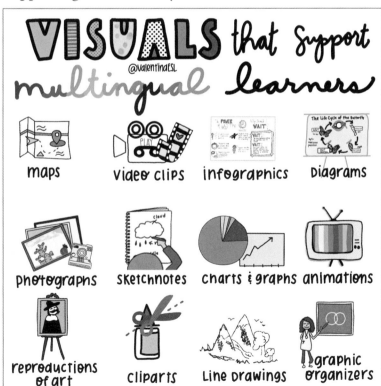

Figure 1–11 Visuals That Support Multilingual Learners

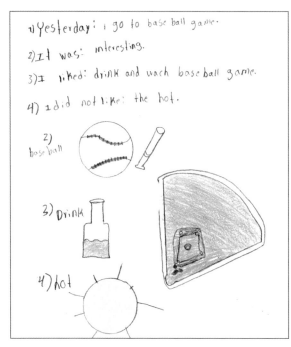

1) Yesterday: i go to base ball game.

2) It was: interesting.

3) I liked: drink and wach baseball game.

4) I did not like: the hot.

2) baseball

3) Drink

4) hot

Figure 1–12 **Student-Created Visuals Support Communication**

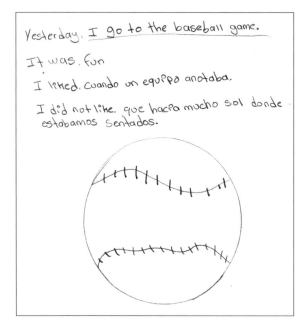

Yesterday, I go to the baseball game.

It was, fun

I liked, cuando un equipo anotaba.

I did not like. que hacía mucho sol donde estabamos sentados.

Figure 1–13 **This Student Used Both Languages and Visual Representation to Support Communication**

Visual support for beginner language learners is a lifesaver. It has been well established that creating a language-rich, vibrant environment significantly contributes to language and literacy development for all students (Gottlieb and Ernst-Slavit 2014). For starting MLs, making language visible is a must, especially when realia are not available for every topic you teach. Look around your classroom and assess ways you can create or enrich the learning environment visually by making illustrated word walls, posting sentence frames for oral and written communication, or enhancing anchor charts or posters. Valentina Gonzalez's poster (Figure 1–11) shows different types of helpful visuals.

Please keep in mind that Figure 1–11 is not intended to be an all-encompassing list. The most important pedagogical purpose of using visuals is to show not just tell what you are teaching about or what your students are learning about—and those two are not always the same: students can be on the receiving end as they work on making sense of or interpreting visuals, or students can be creators or producers of visuals, using them to demonstrate their own understanding or express their ideas or feelings. Figures 1–12 and 1–13 show how two starting level students in Laurie Tucker's high school class chose to respond to the task of sharing about a visit to a baseball game differently: one student chose to add lots of illustrations to more clearly communicate his ideas, while the other used two languages (English and Spanish) and one image to share her experiences.

When it comes to learning tasks or engagement activities, the possibilities are almost endless, so just for the fun of it, I created a short A-to-Z list of ideas on page 28. As you read through these suggestions, keep visualizing what your starting level students can do with the various visuals mentioned in Figure 1–11 and how these tasks fit into your content lessons (and perhaps even benefit all of your students).

Building oracy

Some starting level MLs begin to communicate and participate in the classroom in a relatively short period of time—within weeks, days, or even hours after first being introduced to English. Whenever available, establish language partnerships that represent bilingual peer bridges (pair up the starting level ML with a peer who speaks the same home language but is more proficient in English) to ensure your student has someone to talk to both in the shared language and in English. An important caveat to keep in mind is that you should not use the peer as a translation or interpretation service. Simultaneous translation of instruction by a peer is not a viable or sustainable scaffold; while periodically it can get the message across fast, you must have a range of other strategies ready as well.

The initial verbal expressions to expect from starting level MLs in English are frequently repeated from what they hear you and their classmates say ("Good morning!" "Yes, please!" "No, thank you!" "See you later!") or what they are prompted to say when you offer modeling, gesturing, ample repetition, and support ("My name is _____." "I come from _____." "I am _____ years old."). Next, they are likely to learn formulaic English that goes beyond simple greetings and polite phrases and is more closely connected to the academic discourse in your class. Structured, scaffolded opportunities to add single words to sentence frames will build oral language in MLs.

Adolescent starting level students might be self-conscious about beginning to participate in front of the whole class, so you can choose to make interactions with them more personal rather than public. Here are a few tips on how to periodically work alongside your students at their desks:

→ Check on their work.

→ Ask and answer individualized questions.

→ Encourage them to ask questions and pinpoint what they are struggling with.

→ Offer a few reassuring words.

→ Provide feedback on their progress.

→ Probe them with guiding questions that initially require yes-or-no answers or shorter, readily available responses.

There are so many ways your starting level students *can* share and deepen their thinking. For example:

Add their own sketches or ideas to existing images

Brainstorm titles for images

Create their own visuals to capture important events, people, or places in their lives or their personal goals, interests, and future aspirations

Describe what they see in their home language, English, or both

Evaluate differences and similarities by comparing historical and contemporary images

Find specific details in images or videos

Generate captions for visuals you provide

Highlight important parts of a diagram or graph

Indicate their opinions (likes and dislikes) through visual annotations

Jot down questions they have about an image using their home language, English, or both

Keep a photo or image file (physical or digital) related to key concepts they are learning

Label visuals to name important objects or attributes of the items in the picture

Match images that belong together (or match labels with images)

Name recognizable elements of the image

Outline a photo-essay using images students have located

Practice photojournalism and document a day in their lives in and out of school

Question or quiz each other about images in their home language or English

Record their own videos

Sort images into categories

Tell a narrative via images

Use images in Google slideshows or PowerPoint presentations

View images or videos just for enjoyment

Write notes about the images or videos

X out the image that does not belong in a set of four and explain their thinking

Yell out what they see as the class views an image together

Zoom in on a specific detail in an image, then zoom out to examine the larger context

MLs will begin to speak when there are authentic opportunities to share ideas. What are some ways to add authenticity to the classroom? Try these ideas:

→ Find out what your starting level MLs are mostly interested in or what is really important in their lives: Is it a sport or hobby? Do they have a special skill or talent? Do they work or take care of a sibling? What do they spend their free time doing? Incorporate elements of those special interests into lessons or tasks to make sure your students see themselves in the curriculum you are presenting.

→ Use learning stations where students work in small groups to solve a common problem or contribute to meeting a shared goal. Even if starting level MLs will be at the receptive end of the peer conversation at the onset, they can contribute ideas nonverbally and in their home language in a smaller, safer environment.

Diana Sanchez's biology class supports student learning through kinesthetic and visual tools such as enlarged scaffolded anchor charts. She frequently pairs up English-speaking students and starting level MLs to work together at her anchor chart walls (see Figure 1–14).

In addition to academic learning stations, create interest-based learning opportunities that include your starting level MLs' special interests, skills, and knowledge. You can also invite your starting level MLs to share something about their cultural backgrounds or countries of birth with the class in their home languages (with appropriate translation and interpretation using a peer or tech tool). This will demonstrate to the class the cultural capital and expertise the

Figure 1–14   Everyone Benefits When Working Together

student has, thus increasing their status among peers and opening up opportunities for questions and interactions. Lastly, you can use technology tools (iPad, iPhone videos) to capture the student's utterances and celebrate the progress through weekly recordings (with student and parent permission).

Building foundational reading skills

It is important to distinguish learning the mechanics of reading (letter-sound correspondence, word recognition, managing text structure, and so on) from the language and cognitive demands of reading and developing comprehension (Massaro 2017). For MLs who are nonliterate in their home languages, you need to focus on developing foundational reading skills, which include the ability to

→ demonstrate understanding of basic features of print and the organization of text,

→ know and apply phonics and word-analysis skills to decode words, and

→ understand spoken words and syllables and make connections between sounds (phonemes) and letters representing them.

Other starting level students will not have to start from scratch: they will have varied levels of literacy in their home languages, and they'll be able to transfer many of the well-established skills to English. (Yes, this is true even if their home languages use a different alphabet than English does.) It is imperative to begin teaching reading skills explicitly and systematically to starting level MLs at their current literacy level. Depending on the level of literacy in their home language and the age and grade level of the students, starting level MLs' progression with reading skills may vary significantly. MLs who have advanced literacy skills in their home language may be able to transfer many of the foundational skills, so their reading development may be accelerated.

You should never teach reading to secondary MLs in an isolated, fragmented fashion. Instead, focus your attention to individual needs and relevance to students' lives, interests, and experiences. However, remember to make meaning making and enjoyment key focuses in every literacy lesson for MLs, so as to nurture motivation and interest in developing reading skills. How to achieve this? Here are some strategies you might try:

→ Use a range of prereading strategies that are rich in visuals (pictures, videos, realia, visual concept maps, photographs) to set the stage for understanding the gist of the reading.

- → Preview the text using images or text tours.
- → Use simplified anticipation guides.
- → Use parallel texts that MLs can read in their home language or listen to as audio recordings.
- → Use side-by-side materials: preview the text in their home language, move to English, and then review the material in the home language again.
- → Teach your students how to use Microsoft's Immersive Reader tool.
- → Introduce keywords and use anchor charts or printouts to provide the words for following along.
- → Don't shy away from modeling expressive reading in the secondary classroom but offer meaningful opportunities to stop and process what students are reading or listening to.
- → Read aloud to a small group of students with frequent pauses for comprehension checks.
- → Use digital texts that offer the option of reading aloud to students while they follow along as well as offer multilingual translations.
- → Build a multilingual library and encourage students to use the available resources.

Supporting foundational writing skills

Fluency in English is not a prerequisite to writing. In fact, you cannot wait until MLs develop full language proficiency to begin to write. Copying—although helpful for practicing letter formation—is not meaningful unless the students fully understand what they are copying and have a chance to add their own ideas to the notes. From the day of their arrival, MLs need explicit instruction in writing that combines the mechanics of writing with writing with an authentic purpose, using both the product and the process approaches to instruction. Encourage your starting level MLs to express themselves in writing using their home languages or respond in developmentally appropriate ways using multiple modalities and languages and media. Cummins (2017) suggests integrating writing and sketching for all students when they're exploring nonfiction topics. Starting MLs will especially benefit when they can respond to tasks by sketching, combining speaking and drawing using technological

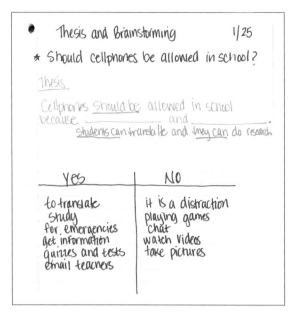

Thesis and Brainstorming   1/25

★ Should cellphones be allowed in school?

Thesis

Cellphones should be allowed in school
because _____ and _____
          students can translate and they can do research.

Yes	No
to translate	it is a distraction
study	playing games
for emergencies	chat
get information	watch videos
quizzes and tests	take pictures
email teachers	

Figure 1–15   Teacher Modeling Followed by
Shared Brainstorming

tools, integrating drawing and writing, listing words and phrases, adding annotations in the language of their choice to drawings they prepared or illustrations you offered, and creating graphic representations of what they have learned or understood in their home language and English.

Middle school ESL teacher Holly Ellis engages her starting and emerging level students in collaborative brainstorming about authentic issues. When her students were working on their persuasive argument text piece, they decided to explore the thesis, "Kids should be allowed to have phones in school" as a group. Holly modeled one reason students should be allowed to have cell phones and one reason why cell phones weren't a good idea in school. Working with partners, students came up with at least five reasons in support of each stance. Figure 1–15 shows one pair's work. Students worked together to translate their work, as five languages are spoken in this class.

For all writing tasks, offer finished models for students to see what your (realistic) expectations are. Whenever possible, also show the process of how to produce the writing you are expecting by modeling the steps. Create an anchor chart or establish peer support to help guide starting level MLs. In addition, model how they can use graphic organizers to record key details in the lesson. See Figure 1–16 for a list of appropriate writing activities.

Figures 1–17 and 1–18 contain work samples from starting level students. Secondary ENL teacher Amanda Haleiko's students keep a personal dictionary to ensure accelerated learning of generic and content-specific vocabulary (see Figure 1–17). Karla Wilder, a secondary educator at a virtual newcomer academy, carefully scaffolds her students' writing. See Figure 1–18 for a student's final product of his illustrated I Am poem.

Technology Integration

Starting level multilingual learners may be at the onset of their language and literacy development in English, but many of them might have advanced technology skills. At the same time, students who have not had access to devices or computers prior

Writing Opportunities for MLs at the Starting Level		
Kind of Writing	**Description/Purpose**	**Tip**
Autobiographical writing	Students can share about their lives, their families, their passions, and their interests.	Offer finished models so students can see what they are working toward as well as templates to follow that clearly indicate what each page may focus on.
Artistic expressions	Students can respond to a task or prompt by creating a visual or artistic response.	Invite students to add words, such as labels, captions, or thought bubbles to combine drawings or other forms of visual arts with words.
Patterned writing	Students can produce a lot of writing even at the Starting level if the basic sentence frame is familiar to them and they can reapply the frame to multiple sentences.	Introduce a sentence frame and use a word wall to scaffold student writing.
Photo projects	Students can create photo collages, montages, or photo essays with or without English or home language text.	Provide print images or have students collect images. If students bring photos from home, offer to make copies so they can keep the original.
Bilingual dialogue journal	Students use both their home language, sketches, and English to communicate with each other or their teachers through a notebook or journal.	If you are bilingual or multilingual, this is a very powerful way to communicate with your students. Respond to the students bilingually, adding a few words in English to sufficiently challenge them.
Personal dictionary	Students look for key words and phrases and create a bilingual glossary with illustrations.	Give MLs a special notebook where they can collect—and develop ownership of—words and phrases they have learned and want to remember.

Figure 1–16

Figure 1–17 Sample Page from a Tenth Grader's Personal Dictionary

Figure 1–18 A Newcomer's Illustrated I Am Poem

to joining your class will need to develop yet another skill set. Technology tools for starting level students can be arranged in three major categories:

1. *Tools to support access to content and language*: Several apps, such as Google Translate, iTranslate, Papago, SayHi Translate, Speak and Translate, TextGrabber, and Waygo, are helpful to translate expressions and short sentences with increasing accuracy from English to just about any language. Figure 1–19 shows one of Sarah Elia's students using Google Translate to scan authentic text and have it automatically translated into their home language. This gives students the opportunity to access higher level texts and have deeper discussions about current events.

   Other web-based resources help teach content through visual input, such as History.com, Discovery.com, Discovery Education, Mathigon, Teach with Movies, the Visual Non-Glossary, and online encyclopedias like Britannica and World Book. These tools support content and language learning.

2. *Tools to support explicit language learning*: There are some well-known apps that can supplement (but never replace) language learning opportunities, such as Rosetta Stone, Duolingo, and Babbel.

3. *Tools to support students' budding language use*: Students find resources to support their word study using sites like Dictionary.com.

Figure 1–19 A Twelfth Grader Reading the Newspaper with the Help of Google Translate. Photo Credit: Adile Jones Photography

They can practice hard-to-pronounce words by doing a simple Google search, adding the word after "pronunciation of." As of the printing of this book, Google provides a wealth of information, such as

→ the phonetic transcription showing which syllable the stress is on

→ an audio recording of the pronunciation in American (or British) English

→ an animation showing how the lips move when pronouncing the word

→ an option to see the word pronounced more slowly

→ an option to record yourself pronouncing the word and get feedback on your pronunciation

Earlier in the chapter I shared a range of different visuals to incorporate into your lessons; Figure 1–20 is a techie version of that list, packed with free resources.

Notice When Starting Level Students Are Ready to Move On

Although most schools determine levels of language proficiency and student placement based on annual standardized assessments such as ACCESS by WIDA, ELPA21, and NYSESLAT, formative assessments and progress monitoring play an important role in your day-to-day work with MLs. To track the progress of starting level students—or all of your students, for that matter—take a multidimensional approach. First and foremost, observe the impact of your own verbal and nonverbal behavior for evidence of comprehension and participation. Take periodic anecdotal records on starting level MLs' participation in instructional activities and social interactions and collect student work samples to document how their written expression is beginning to develop in English.

You will start noticing that starting level students are bridging over to the next language proficiency level when they begin to communicate verbally and in writing, although their linguistic expressions may focus on information they are familiar with (including everyday and routine situations). They will begin to use a string of words, memorized phrases, and short sentences. Their interpretive skills—how much they

Technology Support for Visuals		
Type of Visuals	**One or Two Places Online to Find or Create Them (but definitely look beyond)**	**One Idea on How to Use Them (but definitely go beyond)**
Photographs	Pexels Unsplash	Motivate students with a realistic image
Reproductions of art	National Gallery of Art	Motivate students with an artistic image
Maps	Google Maps MapQuest	Make connections
Animations	Animaker Adobe Animate	Demonstrate how something works
Video clips	ClassHook Pixabay	Tell a story visually
Line drawings	The Noun Project	Quickly capture the essence of a concept
Charts and graphs	Canva Information is Beautiful	Visualize data
Clipart	Clipart Library University of South Florida's ClipArt Etc.	Illustrate objects and ideas with easy to recognize images
Diagrams	SmartArt in Microsoft Word or PowerPoint	Capture connections or relationships between items or to describe functions
Sketchnotes	Notability Goodnotes	Take notes or keep a journal visually
Infographics	Canva Visme Information is Beautiful	Process or present information with minimal text and a collection of images
Graphic organizers	Thinking Maps Tech4Learning's Graphic Organizer Maker	Process or present information showing connections between items

Figure 1–20

understand from what is being spoken or read to them or by them—will exceed their productive language skills, yet you will notice that they begin to ask more questions spontaneously and seem more eager to interact with peers as well. Look out for Amanita as she begins to get around school with ease, makes some new friends, reads at a higher level, and becomes more expressive in speaking and writing. Notice how Fayeq is making every effort to explain his projects and is now describing his work using words and phrases that are growing in length and complexity. You can anticipate that most of your starting level students are going to move beyond the early stages of language acquisition with relative ease and speed!

Chapter Two

Supporting **EMERGING** Level Multilingual Learners

Meet *Emerging* Level Secondary Multilingual Learners

Pedro and Inzali come from different cultural, linguistic, and academic backgrounds, and they attend different secondary schools at different grade levels, yet they both are identified as emerging when it comes to their English language proficiency. As you read about their lives, notice what special experiences and strengths they bring to their classrooms and school communities and how their teachers could intentionally build on these assets (rather than feel frustrated or overwhelmed by perceived challenges and deficiencies). Consider what you would do if Inzali and Pedro or other students with similar experiences were enrolled in your class and how you would support them with their emerging English language skills.

> If a race could be won after the first gallop, thousands would wear blue ribbons.
>
> —AMERICAN FOLK SAYING

Pedro

Like so many others with similar stories, Pedro had a difficult journey crossing the border with a group of other young men, many of whom were barely teenagers. He had to escape El Salvador under dangerous circumstances. His family decided that there was no other choice since he was being actively recruited by local gang members—the only way to survive was to make his way to the United States alone, even though he was only sixteen. After a perilous and exhausting journey, he arrived in Texas, ready for a new life. Unexpectedly, he and some others he vaguely recognized from the trip were put on a bus with others and dropped off in the middle of Washington, DC, not really understanding what was happening. He knew he had some relatives in the New Jersey area, but so much was happening so fast, and his English skills at this point were mainly in the realm of everyday communication. After much delay and with several agencies' support, he was reconnected with his uncle and was enrolled in tenth grade. By this time, it was late October, and the school year had already started.

His high school was nothing like the school he attended prior to coming to the United States. There were so many corridors and wings, and his classes were held in classrooms spread across three floors, so he was grateful when the ELD teacher immediately set him up with a couple of kids who spoke his language (one even had the same county of origin). He learned to manage navigating the building fairly quickly. He got to school early to have breakfast and started attending the extra help periods by his ELD teacher, who always had a friendly, encouraging word for him both in English and in Spanish! Many of his other teachers heard what he'd had to endure and focused on his well-being and found ways to accommodate him: they shared brief outlines of units he missed by not starting the school year in September; they offered brief recorded videos on the school's Canvas website, which was both confusing at first and extremely helpful once he got the hang of it. The math teacher had a Spanish version of the textbook, but it seemed a bit too hard, so Pedro asked for other books in Spanish he could also review. Every day seemed to be a whirlwind for him, and he knew he would have to persevere!

> → STOP AND REFLECT ←
> Pedro had a difficult transitional year after his arrival to the United States and reunion with his extended family members. What can teachers do to support students in similar situations? In what ways could his current school year turn out to be successful? What factors could contribute to that?

Inzali

Now in seventh grade, Inzali was first enrolled in a US school in sixth grade, last year. She is the middle child of three siblings; her older brother, Dedan, is a year ahead of her, and her younger sister, Bennu, is two years behind her. They all arrived together through a refugee resettlement program. Very little is known about her background, but it was disclosed to the school that her father was killed under tragic circumstances and her mother left Myanmar with the three children, first spending time in a refugee camp in Thailand and then finding a new home in the United States. In the regional school system in Vermont, sixth grade was part of the local elementary school, so she had only two core content teachers (one for ELA and social studies and one for math and science) and a language support teacher, who came three or four times a week for a period. Prior to moving to a regional middle school, she took a long time before she began communicating with her teachers or even with her peers. Luckily, a Burmese-speaking family liaison helped the school better understand the trauma she and her family had experienced. Inzali's mother used to be a nurse, and she was quick to find employment as a home health aide, while she also meticulously attended to her children's health and physical well-being. Inzali's middle school ELD teacher and the special subject instructors quickly discovered how gifted she was and paid special attention to nurture her artistic talents. Inzali did not say much, but she drew a lot: sometimes they were doodles, sometimes portraits of beautiful faces she did not want to forget, and sometimes her sketches began to connect to what was being taught. After a year of English language instruction and the coordinated efforts of the core teachers and the ELD specialist, Inzali developed solid foundational skills in English and began to comprehend the grade level content, especially when a range of visual supports were provided. She began to use lots of sketchnotes and other visual tools across all her classes and no longer felt as lost as she did when she first arrived. Since her brother was enrolled in middle school a year before her, she has been able to navigate seventh grade a little bit better and has started to offer more and more encouragement to her little sister, Bennu, who is following in her footsteps.

→ **STOP AND REFLECT** ←
Consider Inzali's family background and determine what assets the family possesses that the school can build upon. What have been Inzali's greatest personal, academic, and familial challenges so far, and how have her teachers been able to address them? What would you do to help Inzali thrive as a multilingual learner if she were in your classroom?

Look Beyond the Label

The word to identify the second level of language acquisition used in this book and in many other contexts—*emerging*—is a powerful descriptor. The name suggests that the learner is leaving behind the first stage and moving into a new level of language development: growing in strength and becoming more communicative. The emerging stage is characterized by students' greater ability to make sense of the world in their new language as well to participate in both social and academic settings at school. Students demonstrate a growing level of comfort with the language, indicated by consistent signs of emergent language production and evidence of participating in classroom activities.

Recently arrived multilingual learners need time to adjust to their new home and school environments. When high school students in Mary Beth Gorman's classroom were reading about immigration and discussing their experiences, many of them chose to capture visually how culture shock impacted them. See Figure 2–1 for one example by a twelfth-grade student.

Keep in mind that multilingual learners function at slightly different levels for the four key language domains (listening, speaking, reading, and writing) as well as when it comes to viewing or visually representing their understandings. Some students could have more facility in a certain domain because of their familiarity with the context, learning preferences, life experiences, interests, motivation, and so on. Some might achieve the emerging level in speaking and listening but not in literacy skills (reading and writing). Other students may demonstrate language at the emerging level in receptive—also called interpretive—skills (listening and reading) but not yet in speaking or writing. As suggested earlier in this book, always consider strategies presented in previous as well as forthcoming chapters, rather than strictly refer to this chapter alone for addressing the needs of emerging level students.

As you'll see in Figure 2–2, the emerging level of language proficiency has other labels, depending on the theoretical framework you refer to, the state or country you live in, or the language development standards you use.

Figure 2–1 A Student Visually Captured Their Feelings of Culture Shock

Other Labels for Emerging Level		
TESOL	**Hill and Miller (2014)**	**WIDA**
Emerging	Early production	Emerging

ELPA (2016)	**New York**	**California**	**Texas**
Emerging	Emerging	Emerging	Beginner

Figure 2–2

Consider What the Research Says

Ofelia García (2009) introduced the term *emergent bilinguals*, or *EBs*, to emphasize rather than diminish MLs' existing language skills and bilingual abilities. In many of her publications, she emphasizes that these students function at home and in their communities in their home languages—creating skills and developing new knowledge and understandings. Students bring these abilities and their home languages and literacies to school, where they learn to acquire a new language and develop English proficiency. Keep in mind that MLs of all ages arrive at school already knowing a great many things that we should value and leverage as we present new skills and knowledge in a new language.

You might be familiar with the concept of translanguaging, which recognizes "linguistic fluidity as the norm" (de los Ríos and Seltzer 2017, 58) for MLs, who can take "flexible and meaningful actions" and "select features in their linguistic repertoire in order to communicate appropriately" (Ramirez and Ross 2019, 178). For example, students may tap into all the languages available to them when they read something in English but discuss the topic with their peers in their shared home languages. *Translanguaging* was originally defined by García (2009) as "an approach to bilingualism that is centered not on languages . . . but on the practices of bilinguals that are readily observable" (45). Further research into this construct reminds us that multilingual students and adults have access to and capitalize on their entire linguistic repertoire constantly, instead of merely communicating in one language at a time and switching back and forth between separate linguistic entities in their brains. So don't shy away from using multilingual materials, and do provide your students with access to core content in their home languages (if they have adequate literacy skills).

More recently, Lucía Cárdenas Curiel and Christina M. Ponzio (2021) reminded us of the promise multimodal and translanguaging practices hold for authentic cultural writing experiences for MLs. They, too, caution us:

> *Often the teacher determines which cultural tools, such as classroom texts or students' linguistic and cultural resources, are invited into the classroom and how they might be adapted to enhance learning. Likewise, teachers may explicitly or implicitly communicate to learners that certain tools are excluded. (83)*

Let's agree that we should value and respect all languages in the classroom rather than narrow language use to one, namely English! When we develop translanguaging pedagogy based on students' authentic language practices, students are able to draw on all their linguistic and cultural resources and more successfully participate in their secondary classes as well.

Understand Emerging Level Secondary Multilingual Learners

Secondary MLs who are recognized to be at the emerging level of language proficiency represent a spectrum of experiences, aptitudes, interests, and skills. Some may have just moved along from the starting level, whereas others may be fast approaching the developing level. Students are likely to understand and process a lot more information through listening, viewing, and reading than they are able to express through speaking and writing. They may successfully comprehend the essential learning that takes place in the classroom.

> *There is nothing wrong with English language learners—no deficit to fix. They are whole students we must reach and teach in ways that open their minds to the amazing possibilities of their lives, and language must not be a barrier to that goal.*
>
> (National Education Association 2015, 19)

Continuing with an assets-based philosophy, let's take a closer look at what emerging level secondary students can do linguistically. Notice how successfully and creatively these students can express themselves. For example, see Figure 2–3 for a student work sample from Jennifer Edwards' high school ELD Level 2 class, where students were preparing to write richly illustrated personal narratives. They were reading *Emmanuel's Dream: The True Story of Emmanuel Ofosu Yeboah* (Thompson 2015) and focusing on direct and indirect characterization. Students sketched Emmanuel as a two-sided character. One side represented how others perceived him, and the other represented how Emmanuel saw himself. Later, students focused on plot and sequence. Each student illustrated (either digitally or by hand) a type of journey from their own life. Many students focused on their immigration journey, but others chose an educational journey, a journey toward a goal, or a map of relationships that had been influential in their lives.

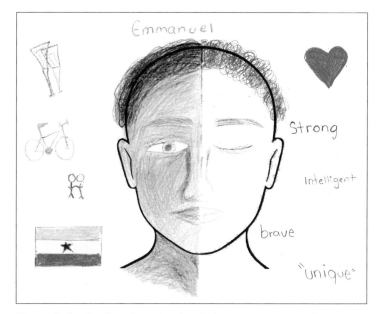

Figure 2–3 Student Drawing Depicting How Emmanuel Was Perceived by Others (Left) and Himself (Right)

When it comes to *listening*, you can expect your emerging level students to begin to show evidence of comprehending what they hear by doing the following:

→ following one- or two-step directions given by the teacher

→ arranging pictures (photos, illustrations) and objects based on oral descriptions

→ drawing or writing in response to simple oral descriptions or commands

→ understanding peer conversations about everyday topics and familiar academic topics

→ understanding the main idea of what you are presenting but possibly missing important details or nuances

→ participating in small-group activities by partially relying on what peers are doing while also figuring out meaning by more closely listening

→ constructing meaning from spoken words with the help of contextual or visual supports

Regarding *speaking* skills, you will notice that emerging level MLs

→ use memorized phrases and sentences with more confidence

→ share more information about themselves

→ use "incomplete sentences and phrases orally to communicate complete thoughts" (Fairbairn and Jones-Vo 2019, 132)

→ express feelings, preferences (likes and dislikes), and opinions in short phrases and simple sentences

→ ask questions about everyday situations and familiar academic content

→ respond to questions with one-word answers, phrases, or short sentences

→ restate what they have heard and understood

→ describe people and objects using pretaught adjectives

→ describe pictures and illustrations presented to them or prepared by them

Figure 2–4 Canva Presentation on a Student-Selected Musical Genre (Banda)

Holly Sawyer, a high school ESL teacher with National Board Certification, integrates culturally responsive instructional practices with technology tools such as Canva in her classes to support her students' multimodal self-expression and digital literacy (you can see one of her students with her work in Canva in Figure 2–4).

Considering *reading*, students at the emerging level are going to be fast to develop some foundational skills and demonstrate increased comprehension, especially if you've made ample visual and multimodal tools available. They will

→ develop basic skills regarding the mechanics of reading

→ understand and retell the main idea of a text, especially if the topic is familiar

- identify key details, especially if they can continue to use visuals, graphs, and other nonverbal elements for understanding
- interpret text features such as title, subtitle, illustrations, captions, and first sentence of each paragraph
- identify key elements of a story, such as characters and setting

As far as their *writing* skills are concerned, emerging level students will

- have acquired most of the foundational skills regarding the mechanics of writing
- continue to label and write short phrases using a growing vocabulary
- continue to illustrate or combine visual representations and writing to express ideas in writing
- use their home language to communicate (if literate in it), including some English words and phrases
- use their home language to help facilitate writing in English, such as brainstorming or outlining ideas
- complete sentence frames that require short phrases
- produce sentences supported with sentence starters or word banks
- begin to write sentences independently
- begin to write short narrative or descriptive pieces
- write about familiar topics (self, preferences, personal experiences, opinions) and academic topics they have mastered with more confidence
- make short annotations (such as text markups) as well as take scaffolded or partially completed notes at their reading levels

Consider what your expectations are for emerging level students. Just like starting level students, they, too, are most likely to succeed and progress when their teachers give support in multiple ways, languages, and modalities. I expect Pedro from the beginning of the chapter to begin to use a range of digital tools for checking understanding (electronic dictionaries), rehearsing his interactions with peers (Flip), navigating cloud-based tools (Canvas and Google), and creating digital texts (Storyboard). He will be able to communicate with his peers with more confidence using both his home language and growing English skills and expand his writing into more complete sentences and paragraphs. For Inzali, my expectations are that she'll continue to use her artistic talents—drawing, sketching, and visually capturing and demonstrating her new understanding—and will attach language to those visual representations with increasing frequency and ease.

Begin Here with Emerging Level Students

Recognize that language and literacy development require time. Even if you cannot bring students to grade level across all core content areas in a short period of time, even if you cannot possibly put language and literacy acquisition into hyperdrive, you can give your students support and a sense of purpose, and you can celebrate their steady progress. Find something personally relevant, something that you have in common with your students, and capitalize on that.

Emerging level students continue to be best supported through teaching practices that are multifaceted linguistically and academically. They need learning activities that allow them to listen to others—both teachers and peers—discuss informal and academic topics. They benefit tremendously from viewing short digital recordings about target topics of instruction. When it comes to contributing to class, emerging level students need opportunities to share their ideas by expressing themselves not just nonverbally, visually, artistically, and through movement, as starting level students do, but through expressive language skills as well. Home language use continues to be a critical bridge to acquiring English and to being a valued, multilingual student in the class and school community.

When you have emerging level students in your class, continue to develop their comprehension and involve them in more active language production. Three successful language and literacy development practices to try are (1) targeted vocabulary instruction, (2) verbal scaffolding as adaptive support, and (3) frequent checking for understanding and monitoring comprehension while supporting student participation and multimodal expression.

Grow Vocabulary Through Targeted Instruction

Emerging level students will benefit greatly from the opportunities you give them to grow their vocabulary. The most important tip to keep in mind is that language acquisition is a natural process, so you must integrate vocabulary throughout the day. Think of your lessons as if they were a beautiful story: every story has a beginning, a middle, and an end, and so does every lesson. There are ways to build vocabulary in all three parts of the lesson instead of front-loading a large number of words or introducing concepts out of context—who could retain so many words in their working memory?

Vocabulary strategies for the beginning of the lesson

Introduce a few carefully selected words or phrases that the students absolutely need to understand for what is upcoming in the lesson. Based on the grade-level content and context, choose one or more of these strategies:

→ Use visual supports such as realia (actual objects) and images (illustrations, photographs, pictures, drawings, video clips) to present the word's meaning nonverbally.

→ Offer user-friendly definitions or explanations and, if meaningful, use mnemonic devices that can help students remember challenging words or concepts. For example, the well-known mnemonic MAIN is used to remember the four main causes of World War I (militarism, alliances, imperialism, nationalism—yes, you can also add a second A for assassination).

→ If possible or if needed, invite home language use to explain complex concepts.

→ If applicable, break down compound words or multipart words into smaller meaningful units (prefix, root, suffix). Point out the word parts as you introduce the words to help MLs see patterns. For example, the prefix *un-* tends to mean "not" or "the opposite of."

Kelly Cray, a high school cultural and language support teacher, often starts her lessons with a hook: In Figure 2–5 she is asking her students to name what she is holding and establish some possible connections between the two objects (flour and flowers). To make the lesson even more memorable, she also shared a personal story about lilacs and passed the flowers

Figure 2–5 The Use of Realia Enriches Learning for All

around so the students could experience the fragrance. And the history connection? Lilacs are not native to the Americas. Colonists, especially the French, brought them over in large quantities.

There might be only a handful of keywords to introduce at the beginning of the lesson, but phrases and language chunks (words that go together) are also very meaningful as long as teachers present them in context and supplement them with visuals or home language support.

Vocabulary strategies to use during the lesson

Revisit the keywords, phrases, and language chunks you previously introduced. In addition, anticipate what additional words or phrases will be important to the lesson and pay attention to moments when your students at the emerging level need clarification or seem lost or confused.

> → Define words when they appear in context or ask your English-proficient students for help with defining a word, describing the word, or making connections for their classmates. (The highest level of learning is when you can teach something, right? Peer support, peer interaction, and peer coaching present a win-win situation for all!)

> → Develop a graphic organizer to reveal connections among words and phrases that may be used across lessons and content areas, such as *human migration* in social studies and *butterfly migration* or *cell migration* in science.

> → Alycia Owen, secondary EAL specialist and coach, recognizes that it is more efficient to contextualize new words and expand such learning into word families than to teach just one new word. Throughout a unit and throughout the entire year, her students create an online glossary to note definitions, parts of speech, and multiple ways to use the target words (see Figure 2–6).

> → Create anchor charts to show the target words in print (with illustrations whenever possible). Figure 2–7 shows an anchor chart designed by secondary EAL educator Jane Russell Valezy to remind her middle schoolers how to make sense of words by relying on the context, their prior knowledge, and visualization strategies.

	Sample Online Glossary			
Noun	Verb	Adjective	Adverb	Notes
analysis— a detailed examination of something	analyze— to examine something carefully		analytically— using careful reasoning and attention to detail	The lab technician completed her analysis of the data. (noun) The teacher asked his students to analyze the graph. (verb) 分析
collaboration— the act of working together	collaborate— to work together on a task	collaborative— produced by two or more people working together	collaboratively— in a way that shows teamwork	合作

Figure 2–6

Vocabulary strategies for the end of the lesson or lesson sequence

Take advantage of the last few minutes of your lesson to review the key learnings with all your students, but especially with MLs, who need opportunities to solidify their conceptual understanding.

→ Connect the target word or phrase to previous experiences in the lesson as you review what the lesson was about.

→ Reinforce the keywords by intentionally using them during lesson closure.

→ If you use a vocabulary journal to capture keywords with emerging

Figure 2–7   Anchor Chart to Support Vocabulary Development

level students, invite them to illustrate their words, add home language annotations, or work on developing ownership of the words.

Elizabeth Choi builds content-specific interactive word walls with her students. See Figure 2–8 for a few examples of student-produced definitions and illustrations.

Students need to see our own enthusiasm for learning new words and using precise academic vocabulary, so our work with vocabulary should span the entire lesson rather than be restricted to the beginning of the lesson and end up being ineffective. Figures 2–9 through 2–11 show this in action: High school ESL teacher Jennifer Edwards modeled how to set a one-word resolution or goal for the New Year. Then, each of her students created a poster with their word and three action steps toward their goal. Jennifer further scaffolded this task by having the students sequence possible sentences explaining their chosen words and their goals further.

Offer Adaptive Verbal Supports and Scaffolds

Try multiple meaningful ways of presenting material to students and remember to paraphrase and *revoice* students' utterances so they can hear their own ideas in a more academic format, in more complete sentences, and with pronunciation that offers verbal

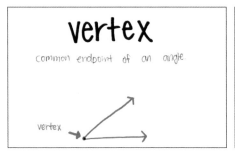
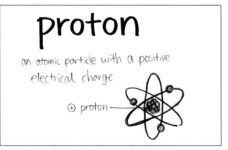

Figure 2–8 **Students Develop Ownership of Complex Concepts with Interactive Word Walls**

Figure 2–9 Teacher Example of a One-Word Resolution

NOURISH
nutrir

I chose this word because I want to focus on caring for my body and soul - for health and happiness

Steps I plan to take to achieve this goal:

#1	#2	#3
Cook more so that I eat less processed food.	Spend more time with friends.	Take more walks in nature.

LEARN

I chose this word because This year I want to learn a lot and not only at school but also from my mistakes and from life.

Steps I plan to take to achieve this goal:

#1	#2	#3
Not make the same mistakes as the previous year	Pay more attention	Learn more English and Practice it

Figure 2–10 Student Poster Depicting a One-Word Resolution

Approximately 80% of New Year's resolutions fail by february. This year, I am choosing a Word of the Year instead of making a New Year's resolution. My word of the year for 2023 is "Learn." I choose this word because this year I want to learn a lot and not only at school but also from my mistakes and from life. There are a few things I am going to do to learn this year. First I will not make the same mistakes as the previous year. This helps me to be better this year. Second I will pay more attention. This will help me learn more things in my classes. Third I will learn more English and practice it. Learning English this year helps me communicate with people and understand my classes. This year I will learn more.

Figure 2–11 Student Explaining Her One-Word Resolution, *Learn*, Through a Scaffolded Paragraph

modeling. Pacheco, Daniel, and Pray (2017) remind us to teach in ways that "support not only students' access to new content and language, but also their participation in an activity where using academic language is a valued classroom practice" (63). Let's agree that academic language is not something students *have* or *do not have*; it is something that all students *use* daily and continue to learn at the level and with the tools available to them. Emerging level students may at times be reluctant to express their ideas, so it is essential to offer adaptive verbal support that includes modeling, redundancy, restating, and extending academic discourse.

Modeling

Modeling can, of course, include using physical models and visuals. You can also model your own thought process by sharing what is going on in your head. For example:

"Let me think about it for a moment" (to show reflection).

"So far, we have discussed . . ." (to show how to summarize).

"Let's take it from the top" (to show how to review or revisit a problem).

"The most important point to remember is . . ." (to show how to synthesize).

Teaching with redundancy

As you speak to your students and describe or explain something, use redundancy and repeat the same ideas in a few different ways. For example, you might introduce the concept of cellular respiration in this way:

Cellular respiration is a chemical process that enables organisms to convert food into energy. During cellular respiration, cells in plants and animals break down sugar and turn it into energy. The purpose of this process is to provide cells with the energy they need to function.

Later in the lesson, you might use redundancy when explaining the equation $C_6H_{12}O_6 + 6O_2$ yields $6CO_2 + 6H_2O$ + energy:

This equation shows that glucose ($C_6H_{12}O_6$) and oxygen (O_2) react to form carbon dioxide (CO_2), water (H_2O), and energy. As the sugar and oxygen react with each other, they release carbon dioxide, water, and energy in the process.

Restating

Restating allows students to hear their thoughts in more formal English. Here are some tips for restating:

→ Try recasting, which is a technical term for repeating what the student said by expanding it and using academic English. (If the student says, "The number on the top is bigger than the one on the bottom," acknowledge this observation and recast the sentence as "You are right, when you work with improper fractions, the numerator will be bigger than the denominator.")

→ Use synonyms for what MLs have said so they can hear their own ideas in a more sophisticated way. (If the student uses the adjective *important* in a sentence describing events that led to the Revolutionary War, you can affirm their ideas and switch *important* to *significant* in your sentence.)

→ Avoid overcorrecting errors your emerging level students make in their oral or written discourse, whether the errors are related to grammar, pronunciation, syntax, or vocabulary. Instead, offer *error feedback* on only the errors that interfere with meaning by asking students for clarification. ("I think I heard you say _____" or "Is that what you meant?")

Extending student talk

Teach classroom discourse moves. Prompt students to build on short phrases or sentences by asking, "Can you tell me more about that?" "That was a really great idea; can you explain it more?" or "What else can you add to that?"

One additional way you can support your students' emerging oral language skills is to not settle for "I don't know." Pam Schwallier, director of EL and bilingual programs, uses a poster like the one shown in Figure 2–12 to remind students of alternative phrases to use when they are unsure of an answer. The poster is based on Seidlitz Education's "What to Say Instead of I Don't Know" stems, a cornerstone of the *7 Steps to a Language-Rich, Interactive Classroom* (Seidlitz and Perryman 2021, 13).

Check for Understanding and Monitor Student Comprehension

Although all students benefit from frequent monitoring, MLs at the emerging level of English language proficiency are often at the cusp of understanding what teachers are presenting and discussing, so your vigilance and response to whether they get it or not is critical. Teachers are data gatherers and problem

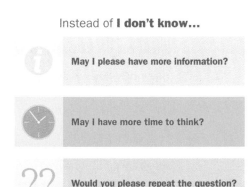

Instead of **I don't know...**

May I please have more information?

May I have more time to think?

Would you please repeat the question?

May I ask a friend for help?

Figure 2–12 Alternatives to "I Don't Know"

From *7 Steps to a Language-Rich, Interactive Classroom,*
by J. Seidlitz and B. Perryman (p. 13). Copyright © 2021
by Seidlitz Education. Reprinted with permission.

solvers, always striving to be "flexible and responsive to students' ever-changing assets and needs. This involves a focus on high level goals, our students, and the ever-changing 'just-right' instruction" (Singer and Staehr Fenner 2020, 63). When you check for understanding, keep in mind that all learners, especially emerging level MLs, will demonstrate what they know and can do in multiple ways and multiple modalities, so allow them to use all their available resources to do so. The challenge faced by teachers of MLs is not only to gather meaningful formative assessment data and monitor MLs' progress through a range of strategies and tools (see seminal work by Fisher and Frey [2014], Gottlieb [2021], and Heritage [2022]) but to ensure that students thrive and accumulate new learning by *acting* on feedback they get (Almarode, Fisher, and Frey 2022; Stiggins et al. 2020).

Observe

Look for nonverbal signals from your students. Both casual and closer, more carefully planned observations of MLs will provide valuable information (Heritage 2022). Watch for nonverbal cues when students do not seem to understand, such as facial expressions, gestures, body language, and restlessness. Use hand signals such as thumbs-up or thumbs-down to quickly gather student responses to yes-or-no questions or when students need to indicate their choices between two answers. Try some commonly applied response tools such as erasable whiteboards or engaging technology tools such as AnswerGarden or Menti to invite participation (see more on technology integration and digital scaffolding later in the chapter).

Assign quickdraws or quickwrites

Use index cards or sticky notes for students to quickly respond to a prompt by jotting down keywords, writing in their language of choice, or creating a drawing that reflects their current understanding. You can embed a quickdraw or quickwrite activity at any point in the lesson: to preassess what students know, to check on how they develop new skills and understandings, or as an exit slip or ticket to leave. Michelle Land, a secondary ESL teacher, frequently invites her students to capture first impressions of a new novel or a new chapter on sticky notes and to create collaborative posters. See Figure 2–13 for three of her students' very different renditions of *Frankenstein* after the class read the first chapter.

Focus on Multidimensional Strategies

Following is a selection of multidimensional instructional practices and strategies for supporting emerging level students, organized into four main strands: (1) social-

Figure 2–13 Students' Reactions to *Frankenstein*

emotional support; (2) experiential learning support; (3) support across multiple modes of communication (including supporting visual literacy, building oracy, and building literacy); and (4) technology integration. Keep in mind that you can use many of these strategies with all levels of language proficiency, so as you read through the book, try to avoid limiting your strategy use to the designated language proficiency level where the strategy is first introduced.

Social–Emotional Support for Adolescent MLs

Emergent level multilingual learners might be new to the country or to their middle or high school, so many of the suggestions in Chapter 1 may also be applicable to this group. Continue to make your students feel welcome, get to know them, and build or strengthen your relationship with the students, their families, and their extended linguistic and cultural communities. Earlier in this chapter, I shared how Jennifer Edwards' students applied direct and indirect characterization to Emmanuel, the protagonist in a story they were reading. As a follow-up, she also invited her students to create self-portraits in the same fashion. See Figures 2–14 and 2–15 for two examples of how students perceived themselves and how others perceived them, revealing students' complex identities and internal struggles.

Establish structures and routines

Structures and routines offer secondary students much-needed consistency and familiarity, which is especially important for those adolescents whose lives have been disrupted. When students experience chronic stress and anxiety and when normalcy disappears from their daily lives, schools and classrooms must provide a safe learning environment and predictable learning opportunities to all. A well-structured class

Figure 2–14 Student Self-Portrait 1

Figure 2–15 Student Self-Portrait 2

period will have learning activities that are readily associated with the beginning, middle, and end of the lesson, such as presented in Figure 2–16.

A well-managed learning environment will have agreed-upon rules and norms and minimal disruptions and distractions. Figure 2–17 shows some classroom rules Alycia Owen cocreated with her students during the first week of school. After

ROUTINES		
Beginning of Lesson	**Middle of Lesson**	**End of Lesson**
bell-ringer activities	teacher-directed lesson presentations	review and summary tasks
reviews of previous learning		student-generated questions
posted agendas and objectives	guided learning activities in a whole group or small groups	exit slips
homework checks	student-led inquiry	tickets to leave

Figure 2–16 Routines for the Beginning, Middle, and End of a Lesson

brainstorming, the class came to a consensus on four expectations, which Alycia posted in the classroom and everyone signed.

Recognize students' need to belong

Adolescent multilingual learners' academic, language, and literacy development heavily depend on their social-emotional well-being. Michelle Lawrence (n.d.), a high school ELL teacher in Buffalo, New York, explains:

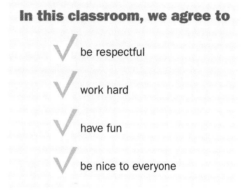

Figure 2–17 Consensus About Classroom Behavior

> *ELLs want to fit in with their American peers, but at the same time they want their identities and cultures validated. This is an ongoing, internal struggle for most students. This struggle may also follow them home where their desire to adopt certain U.S. cultural values clashes with their parents' desire to uphold their own traditional values.*

In your classroom (as well as outside your classroom, in the hallways, cafeteria, schoolyard, and beyond), look out for evidence of such struggles and lessen the stress that your students experience by making a sincere effort to understand them in their full humanity, listening to them without judgment, asking questions without prying, and building strong rapport with them without overstepping boundaries.

Focus on engagement through ownership of challenging but well-supported learning

When examining what types of engagement lead to ownership of deep learning, Ron Ritchhart and Mark Church (2020) point to "engagement with others, engagement with ideas, and engagement in action" (8). Ritchhart and Church might not have been thinking about emerging level adolescent MLs, but you and I are! Let's consider how these three approaches are applicable to English language and literacy development:

> → *Engagement with others*: Emerging level multilingual learners must engage in meaningful exchanges with their teachers and classmates. Learning takes place in a social-constructivist context complete with teacher and peer support.

> → *Engagement with ideas*: When you give your students ample opportunities for deep thinking—reflecting, reading, writing, listening, speaking, viewing, visually representing, and actively interacting with complex ideas in other ways—they develop new conceptual understandings and learning processes as well as new ways of using language connected to these processes.

> → *Engagement in action*: Finally (or perhaps first and foremost), the connections you make between your emergent MLs' lived experiences and their new learning are valuable. As learning becomes more personally relevant and physically engaging, language and literacy usage become more authentic, and as a result, your students develop their agency.

Experiential Learning Support

Learning in an authentic manner in a real-world context is nothing new. Among many others, Washor and Mojkowski (2013) have made a compelling case for increasing student engagement through out-of-school learning experiences. They suggest that "schools must take down the walls that separate the learning that students do, and could do, in school from the learning they do, and could do, outside" (xvii). Martínez-Álvarez (2017) suggests creating hybrid curricular and instructional spaces, in which students document out-of-school experiences with digital photographs and draw from these experiences for in-school projects, such as oral and digital storytelling, writing, and performing. Firsthand experiences such as visits to local museums, science labs, outdoor ecological spaces, or places much farther away from home, such as the backstage area of a Broadway theatre in New York City or the Smithsonian museums in Washington, DC, not only engage students for the day but may have a life-changing impact. These opportunities undergird the asset-based approach, leveraging life experiences, no matter the language in which they occur.

Field trips

Field trips have long been recognized as unique learning experiences for all students (Greene 2016). Important related research has documented that students who saw live theatre demonstrated "enhanced knowledge of the plot and vocabulary in those plays, greater tolerance, and improved ability to read the emotions of others" (Greene et al. 2015, 55). Similarly, students who visit an art museum not only develop more knowledge about art but also "have stronger critical-thinking skills, exhibit increased historical empathy, display higher levels of tolerance, and have a greater taste for consuming art and culture" (Greene, Kisida, and Bowen 2014, 80). Visiting live performances and art museums has positive outcomes on all students, but it is especially powerful for emerging level MLs, who gain authentic cultural and linguistic experiences from carefully planned field trips.

In New Hampshire, middle school EL and social studies teacher Alice Saville takes her students on field trip experiences at Massabesic Audubon Center, where they learn about the local environment and wildlife. They then compare the environment and wildlife to that of their home countries. Alice shared, "We support the student's ability to talk about the things they learn through the study of vocabulary, bird anatomy, visual and aural identification of local birds, as well as the use of binoculars and the internet to find information." Figure 2–18 shows a group of Alice's students discussing their observations during the second field trip, when students use binoculars to identify birds by their markings, behaviors, and the sounds they make. Using a bird identification application and field guides, each student makes notes into a journal and identifies the birds they observe.

Field trips without leaving the school or the vicinity

Whenever you encounter logistical constraints or post-COVID limitations, consider in-class or in-school authentic learning experiences via guest speakers, including parent and community volunteers, assemblies, demonstrations, performances, and in-school field trips. Another option for local, easy-to-implement experiences is micro field trips (Schwartz 2020), which allow you to take the students around campus buildings (especially if you have a large,

Figure 2–18 A Field Trip Gives Students Authentic Learning Experiences

sprawling school property), to sports fields, or to a local park within walking distance of your school building. If your middle school and high school are in adjacent buildings, it can be beneficial for students to see what the other building looks and feels like.

Virtual field trips

With increasing use of technological tools and web-based learning opportunities, remember to open up the world to your students through virtual field trips to major historical sites, museums, and galleries, from Ellis Island to the Anne Frank House, the Metropolitan Museum of Art, the Smithsonian Institution, Plimouth Patuxet Colony, and more. Incorporating Google Earth into the experience will allow your students to travel to the destinations you select for your virtual field trip, gliding across states, countries, or continents. Teacher Mariel Gómez de la Torre-Cerfontaine regularly takes her students on virtual trips. Then they use WriteReader to turn their virtual experiences into digital books. See Figure 2–19 for some sample pages from one of her students' books about a virtual visit to Denmark.

This is our guest speaker. His name is Mr. Babar Baigs. He is the CEO of WriteReader App. It is located in Denmark. We were so lucky, because he accepted to give us a tour by bicycle to show us Copenhagen which is the capital of Denmark.

Mr. Baigs was showing us the Danish Parlament. It looks different from the USA parlament. It is totally open to the public.

Figure 2–19 Sample Pages from a Student-Created Digital Book About a Virtual Field Trip

Connections between real-life experiences and language and literacy development

What happens before, during, and after the field trip or other authentic cultural and linguistic experience? How you prepare the students for the experience, guide them throughout, and then process and reflect on what students have seen and done are important details to make it a success and to significantly contribute to language and literacy development. See Figure 2–20 for some guidelines on how to maximize the impact of authentic learning experiences.

Alice Saville, middle school EL and social studies teacher, is mindful of how learning continues after a field trip is over. To connect to their personal experiences,

Activities to Do Before, During, and After Field Trips	
Before a Field Trip or Other Authentic Experiences	• Build up excitement about the forthcoming activity. • Generate questions. • Have students make predictions. • If students wish to share similar life experiences they had in another country or context, give them opportunities to do so.
During a Field Trip or Other Authentic Experiences	• Set up partnership teams (two or three students participating together) to help them engage in authentic conversations and meaningful use of social and academic language. • Create a task that helps anchor these authentic learning experiences: have students take digital photos, use a note-catcher template or app to take notes, audio-record their observations, or video-record short examples of the experience.
After a Field Trip or Other Authentic Experiences	• Have students co-construct a short narrative with each other or with you. • Use notes, photographs, and digital audio or video recordings to engage in in-class speaking and writing activities: ask students to describe locations and people, recall details, sequence events, and identify similarities and differences of experiences. • Create photo essays, digital posters, or newsletters documenting the experience: have Emerging level MLs identify and write captions or add other annotations to accompany the photographs.

Figure 2–20

Figure 2–21 Student Drawing of a Turquoise-Browed Motmot

Figure 2–22 Student Preparing a Presentation on Hawks

her students research and illustrate a bird that is common to their country of origin. (See Figure 2–21 for a drawing of a bird native to El Salvador by one of her students.) During another post-field-trip activity, students research either a bird they saw at the Audubon center or a bird indigenous to New Hampshire and create a slideshow of photos and videos of the bird along with facts of the bird's habitat, behavior, and color variation (see Figure 2–22 for another student from her class, who studied and presented on hawks). Alice is very proud of her students' accomplishments. She shared, "These activities help my students develop research and design skills and give them opportunities to use English successfully in an academic setting."

Support Across Multiple Modes of Communication

Emerging level adolescent multilingual learners may be excited or frustrated with their efforts to communicate. Supporting them to express themselves across visual and other nonlinguistic modalities as well as scaffolding their participation in oral language uses and academic literacy tasks are essential steps to ensure their continued confidence with their new language and their success in your classroom.

Supporting visual literacy

One way to foster visual literacy is the picture word inductive model, or PWIM. This strategy is not new to many classrooms (Calhoun 1999; Ferlazzo and Sypnieski 2022). Its recent resurgence may be attributed to its versatility because it supports visual literacy as well as students who heavily rely on visual modality. In several phases, you elicit words through large- or small-group brainstorming activities, analyze the words, and help students formulate sentences as they observe and discuss a large picture. They can attach words and phrases to the picture, engage in discussions about it, sort and classify the words they collectively gather, write about the image, and suggest a title that could best describe the picture. If you have never tried PWIM, you might want to use it when assessing background knowledge early in a unit or perhaps in generating interest around a new concept. You may also try it when introducing complex concepts directly using visual input first. See Figure 2–23 for an example of an image that could open a discussion of the gold rush and the role Chinese immigrants played in completing some of the most dangerous construction jobs of the time. The picture, taken of the White Pass and Yukon Route railway in Alaska, offers not only a breathtaking view but also opportunities for questions and inquiry. The PWIM strategy is very versatile, and pictures like this are helpful to put historical events into perspective.

You can also try visual thinking strategies (VTS). All students benefit from lessons that integrate VTS; however, you will find that learning through visual modalities is especially beneficial to emerging level MLs in developing complex understandings. VTS was originally designed to engage students in close examination of complex visual texts; the process resembles close reading of written texts (Yenawine 2013). You can incorporate a variety of visual texts into each lesson, as long as the visuals

Some nouns:
mountain
valley
trees
rocks
trestle
train
train tracks
engine
cars

Some adjectives:
tall
beautiful
dangerous
scary

Some questions for discussion:

Where was this picture taken?

When were the train tracks built?

How did they build train tracks so high up on the mountains?

Why did they build this railroad?

Figure 2–23   A Variation of the PWIM Strategy

are aligned to the instructional goals, they represent the complex ideas you want to teach, and they help contextualize vocabulary (Capello and Walker 2016). In social studies, for example, historical photographs taken during the Great Depression lend themselves to developing conceptual understanding and provide a unique opportunity to attach descriptive language to iconic images. In biology, you might use stunning photographs like those found in the "Biology in Pictures" section of the American Institute of Biological Sciences website to explore recent discoveries visually with your students.

Ask emerging level MLs to begin by generating a list of what they recognize and can readily identify in the picture; however, it is more engaging and enriching if the image invites students to make predictions and interpret, not just describe, what they see. Share some pictures you have taken or encourage students to bring in their own pictures to make this activity even more personalized.

Building oracy

Emerging level MLs are ready for interaction, so position them as thinkers and valuable contributors to the class community. It is widely accepted among educators that speaking and listening skills are directly connected to reading and writing skills, and all four modalities together help nurture thinking skills. Students in the secondary school context may be more reserved and less likely to openly share and let their voices be heard. However, Tracy G. Spies and Yunying Xu (2018) remind us that students will show higher levels of risk-taking and engagement when they "feel safe, valued, and respected, as this allows students to respond, contribute, and participate in learning" (224). Errors are to be expected and accepted—by all: multilingual learners, classmates, teachers, and parents alike. But let's keep in mind that, as Minkel (2018) observes, "a twelve-year-old English learner is capable of the same complexity of thought, innovative ideas, and profound questions" as their English-proficient peers—even if their speaking abilities in their new language still have to catch up with their thinking abilities.

So, how can we nurture oracy among MLs? Universal prompts—as suggested by Bambrick-Santoyo, Settles, and Worrell (2013)—will help facilitate oral language development in all students. The more MLs hear their teachers apply prompts such as "What makes you think that?" "Why do you say so?" and "Why is this important?" to elicit more student talk, the more likely it is that MLs will internalize and use these talk moves with their peers or even as they reflect on their language use and self-expression.

Try this strategy for oracy support: One-on-one time   Giving students undivided attention is difficult, but if you have students engage in learning stations or independent work, you can open up a help desk or a conferring corner and find one-on-one time with students. Deconstructing a challenging task, offering a visual prompt, or engaging in a text- or content-based discussion with students will not only build relational trust with them but give them much-needed targeted modeling of language use. In addition, teacher-led small-group discussions allow for MLs at the emerging level to benefit from dialogic teaching and hearing their peers contribute their ideas.

Pair conversations or peer interaction   A well-established strategy for student interaction is called think-pair-share (Lyman 1981), which might be more commonly used at the elementary level but is just as effective and powerful with adolescents (even adults!). First, students receive a prompt related to the topic of instruction. Then they each think about the prompt on their own. Next, they pair up and share their ideas with their partner. For example, the teacher might ask students to think about all the reasons we should protect endangered animals. Students would first think of as many reasons as they could individually before sharing their reasons with others.

Think-pair-share is one of the most powerful techniques for academic oral language development, especially when this strategy is also connected to reading or visually interpreting information (Robertson n.d.). You can ask students to individually read a selection assigned to them, watch a short video clip, or reflect on a question you've presented, then pair up to discuss their ideas, and finally share their ideas. There are lots of options for tailoring this strategy to your instruction (see Figure 2–24).

Emerging level students can successfully participate when we offer sentence starters or oral language development stems.

Think, Pair, Share		
Think	**Pair**	**Share**
Context for thinking: • For thirty seconds • For one minute • While jotting ideas down • While sketching or drawing • While annotating text	**Structure for conversation with partner:** • Agree or disagree • Share experiences • Share opinions • Share reactions • Explain perspectives	**Options for sharing out:** • Within pairs • In small groups of four (by doubling up the pairs) • In larger groups • As a whole class • Using technology (such as polling tools)

Figure 2–24

Triad talks   As the name suggests, triads go beyond pair work and require the formation of groups of three. Preassign groups of three students that will include one emerging level ML and two other students at higher language proficiency levels. Have them work together multiple times throughout the week for continuity.

The triads provide support as students rehearse their responses before sharing out to their whole class. Teach students to include everyone in the conversation by asking each other to add something or clarify their response, to provide evidence to support their claims, or simply to share what they are thinking.

Supporting emerging reading

Read-alouds are not just for the elementary classroom (Calderón and Slakk 2018). Students in all grade levels and all proficiency levels benefit from them; yet emerging level MLs who do not read complex texts in English on their own or cannot read with the fluency necessary for comprehension (yet) benefit even more! They can be more successfully exposed to literature (both fiction and nonfiction) through read-alouds.

In the context of elementary education, Jim Trelease (2019) reminds us that "we read to children for all the same reasons we talk with children: to reassure, to entertain, to bond, to inform or explain, to arouse curiosity, and to inspire" (6). Secondary students can equally benefit from strategic read-alouds (Van Der Wende 2021). Listening to adults read aloud has a range of positive outcomes for students of all ages, especially for emerging level MLs:

> → It helps students build receptive vocabulary.
>
> → It adds to their active vocabulary.
>
> → It associates reading with a joyful experience.
>
> → It motivates students to read or explore new topics introduced through the read-aloud.
>
> → It promotes critical thinking.
>
> → It fosters community building in the classroom.
>
> → It makes MLs more excited about trying to read on their own (text tours, previews, skimming, and scanning are all welcome steps for emerging level MLs).

In addition to helping students with their oral language development, brief read-alouds to the whole class or smaller groups of students also contribute to building a community of learners and a sense of belonging (Miller 2013). Read-alouds significantly contribute to language acquisition and they also help students create background knowledge about topics they do not have personal experience with. You can honor MLs' lived experiences if you choose readings that reflect their cultural backgrounds. Finally, read-alouds provide emerging level MLs and many of their classmates with a reading role model.

Through read-alouds, you invite your students into your literary life by sharing something you read in the news, a recent discovery in a science journal, a book or movie review you came across, an excerpt from a novel, a poem by a poet laurate, and so on. When you pause to ask questions or think out loud about the text—also referred to as think-alouds or comprehend-alouds (see Chapter 4)—students develop new appreciation for reading being an active process. When your students have recurring opportunities to listen to you or a more proficient classmate read aloud, you can

Figure 2–25 A Student Explores the Read-Aloud from the Day

count on multiple outcomes: MLs will improve their listening skills, model their own emerging reading skills after you, and emulate your reading behaviors while their academic stress will be lessened. Junior high school science teacher Diana Sanchez frequently reads aloud to her students at the start of her lessons. She has noticed many of her emerging level students using her comfortable classroom library to reread the books she has read aloud (see Figure 2–25).

Following are some tips for a successful read-aloud.

→ Ensure all students are ready to hear your reading of the text.

→ Show sincere curiosity for the material: if you are excited to read, the feeling will be contagious.

→ If appropriate, spend some time previewing the text—take a quick visual or textual tour.

→ Read with expression.

→ Adjust the pacing by using clear annunciation, adequate pauses, and appropriate facial expressions and gestures.

→ Encourage students to create mental images as you read, and model how to visualize something by describing what you see. For emerging level students, sketch out your visualization or share images or photographs.

> $\rightarrow$ Pause to share your thinking about the text, or invite your
> students to share their thinking to
>
> - make predictions,
> - ask and answer questions,
> - describe characters,
> - build theories about the reading, or
> - reflect on key details in the text.

For greater impact, find ways to have your MLs reread the same text or an extension of the text you shared with them. Whenever possible, surround read-alouds with rich, authentic conversations. Record yourself and save the read-aloud digitally or make the material available to the students in print or digital format for repeated, multimodal access to the material.

Supporting emerging writing

When we maximize MLs' cultural experiences and existing language skills, we can expect more positive outcomes (Snyder and Staehr Fenner 2021). One way to achieve this is to continue to invite emerging level students to write both socially and academically and to use their home languages for brainstorming, drafting, or expressing their ideas in writing. Inviting them to add to their thoughts in English will bridge the languages available to them.

Consider the following updated suggestions based on Cummins' (2005) work to make meaningful connections between students' home languages and English:

> $\rightarrow$ Draw attention to the cognates that exists in the students'
> home languages and English, thus raising their metalin-
> guistic awareness regarding relationships across languages
> (as well as awareness about false cognates: not all words
> that look or sound the same in two languages mean
> the same).
>
> $\rightarrow$ Have students respond to tasks by transferring their ideas
> from the initial language of writing (such as their home lan-
> guage) to English.
>
> $\rightarrow$ Invite multimedia and multilingual projects that honor all the
> languages the students can use as well as multiple modali-
> ties that stretch beyond the traditional definitions of literacy
> (e.g., iMovies, PowerPoint presentations, Prezis).

> → Initiate shared learning experiences across your own school or campus or create "sister class projects where students from different language backgrounds collaborate using two or more languages" (Cummins 2005, 588).

In their seminal work, Patricia Velasco and Ofelia García (2014) recognize that translanguaging may be used in all phases of the writing process, including the planning, drafting, and final production stages. Students can take notes in one language and finish a project in another, or they can utilize both of their languages and create and illustrate bilingual reports to use their full linguistic repertoires as well as visual tools for expression.

Similarly, capitalize on students' ability and willingness to express themselves through nonlinguistic representations, such as communicating their ideas via sketchnotes, drawings, diagrams, graphic organizers, outlines, or mixed modalities that integrate written words with illustrations. Digital or traditional scrapbooking encourages student self-expression (Weinstein 2021); as students gather textual and visual artifacts around a theme, they can generate a collection of items in a photo album or a digital platform such as Mixbook. Invite them to label heavily and write short captions for each item in their scrapbooks. Emerging level MLs will enjoy writing about topics they have more knowledge about and experience with, and they will benefit from the writing supports you plan for them. See Figure 2–26 for a sketchnote Elizabeth Choi's middle school student created as he was learning about plot diagramming.

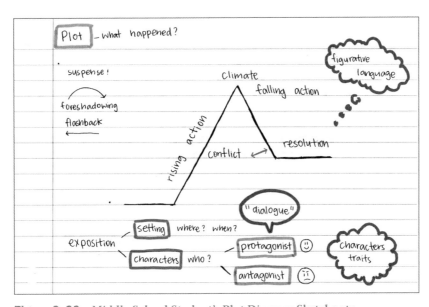

Figure 2–26 Middle School Student's Plot Diagram Sketchnote

Here are some tips to help emerging level students be successful with writing:

→ Engage students in rich conversations to prepare them for writing.

→ Spend more time on prewriting and drafting by offering scaffolds, outlines, word banks, and "feedforward" (guidance that helps students with next steps) instead of only giving after-the-fact feedback.

→ Structure writing tasks into shorter, more manageable subtasks.

→ Offer step-by-step directions and accessible samples (exemplars or models).

→ Guide student writing with frequent questions and prompts.

→ Offer sentence frames and sentence starters.

→ Supply a word bank or phrase bank that is comprehensible to the students at this level.

→ Support writing with visuals, diagrams, or pictures.

→ Confer with students to provide ongoing support and feedback.

Technology Integration

Many digital tools are well suited for emerging language expression and—from the teacher's perspective—for student work sampling. As your students get engaged in all four domains (listening, speaking, reading, and writing) via digital tools, you can use these platforms for gathering anecdotal records along with authentic written work samples or oral language samples from your students. Notability is one app that allows you to capture your own notes along with photographs of students or their work or even video clips of students' participation. For oral language samples, a simple iPhone or iPad digital recording will do, or have students digitally record themselves as they explain their ideas or present their work via Flip. Figure 2–27 summarizes the benefits of using digital tools for several key instructional practices.

How Digital Tools Can Enhance Instruction

Instructional Practice	Digital Tools	How Do They Help?
Multimedia presentations/ response	Padlet, Nearpod, VoiceThread	Students watch (and eventually create) multimodal presentations.
Digital recordings	Screencastify, Loom	Students watch short lessons to glean essential learning.
Digital story telling	Book Creator, Adobe Spark	Students become producers, not just consumers of digital and multimodal text.
Web-based reading materials (e-books, blogs)	Newsela, Newsinlevels	Students access, high-interest levelled reading materials.
Digital whiteboards	Jamboard, Witeboard	Students brainstorm and collaborate.
Web-based learning games	Kahoot, Gimkit	Students learn through game-like activities.
Digital recording for oral response	Flipgrid, EdPuzzle	Students rehearse oral responses (record and rerecord as needed).
Student and parent messaging tools	Talking Points, Remind, WhatsApp	Students and families are informed.

Figure 2–27

Notice When Emerging Level Students Are Ready to Move On

Although most schools determine levels of language proficiency and student placement based on annual standardized assessments, such as ACCESS by WIDA, ELPA21, and NYSESLAT, they are conducted many months prior to the new academic year, so the results might already be outdated when you begin to work with your students. Therefore, formative assessments and progress monitoring play a critical role in your day-to-day, week-to-week, and month-to-month work with MLs. To track the language and literacy development progress your emerging level students make, consider your ongoing observations of how the students are doing in your classroom not just with core content attainment but with their use of language and literacy embedded in the subject matter. Make sure you frequently check in and collaborate with your other subject area colleagues and ESOL or ELD specialists, who are likely to have a comprehensive approach to progress monitoring and will be ready to share insights about your students. Consider combining evidence of student learning obtained from multiple sources and representing multiple perspectives—including teacher observations of oracy (listening and speaking), student work samples that document how their writing skills have developed, and periodic individual conferences where you can check on their comprehension and also monitor how their disciplinary reading skills are growing. You will be amazed by most of your students' relatively fast initial growth before the rate of language development tapers off somewhat (remember the principle *lower is faster; higher is slower*), so maximize this growth for your students in every possible way!

You will start to notice that students at the emerging level are bridging over to the next language proficiency level when you can elicit longer answers from them and observe them participating in more complex conversations. For both Pedro and Inzali, single-word answers or short phrases will turn into sentences as they begin to offer more, give some examples, add more details, describe a person or object mentioned, or try to explain their thinking further. Pedro's and Inzali's reading fluency and comprehension will increase and their writing will reveal how phrases and short sentences start fitting together into more extensive forms of expression.

Chapter Three

Supporting DEVELOPING Level Multilingual Learners

Meet *Developing* Level Secondary Multilingual Learners

Let's meet Galyna and Mateo, two students who are at the developing level of second language acquisition. They have reached the intermediate level in their expressive language skills, yet their academic language development (as well as their social-emotional development) requires careful support to ensure success and continued growth. As you read their stories, see if you recognize these experiences in your own students. If you have had MLs with similar backgrounds and responses to schooling in the United States, consider what you would do to ensure a productive year for them.

You can't see the whole sky through a bamboo tube.

—JAPANESE PROVERB

Galyna

Galyna was born and grew up in Ukraine. Her family escaped through Poland in the early days of the Russian invasion, but they did not arrive in Ohio, one of the largest refugee resettlement centers in the United States, until close to six months later. The spring of her seventh grade was a blur. The shock of leaving her extended family and friends behind in a hurry seemed to have washed over everything, so for the first time in her life, Galyna was not excited to prepare for the new school year. Her parents were concerned that she would not be able to shed the trauma without much ongoing family and community support. In Ukraine, she was a cheerful, dreamy preteen who loved reading—*The Hunger Games* (Collins 2008) was one of her most recent favorites. She loved languages, having studied Russian in school and English in an after-school program, with a primary focus on reading and translating between languages.

When Galyna began eighth grade in Cleveland, she was classified as an English learner at level three. She was a conscientious student, and it was evident that both she and her family valued school. Because she had excellent literacy skills in her primary language, her parents anticipated that her English language development would progress consistently. She used to enjoy school back home, but her family had a hard time locating reading materials in the middle of the chaos that dominated their lives for months. Instead, Galyna turned to her phone, and now TikTok, YouTube, and other platforms seemed to occupy all her time. Her parents were worried and some of her teachers shared that concern. Her ESOL teacher, Ms. Perez, began to use a dialogue journal with a handful of her students, including Galyna. Ms. Perez found that the dialogue journal, a personalized notebook that remained at school and was shared between the student and the teacher, could help build a relationship with her students and provide a safe avenue for sharing while also practicing writing daily.

The dialogue journal entries not only revealed that Galyna was struggling with making sense of the world but also gave insights into how she was developing her writing skills. Based on Ms. Perez's confidential recommendation, the school-based support team set up regular meeting times with Galyna to initiate a trauma-responsive intervention. Regarding her formal and informal writing, a common pattern emerged showing that she preferred to produce short, well-formed sentences without taking much risk with more grammatically complex structures. She defaulted to the present tense even when describing something that happened in the past. Although she had acquired a sizeable vocabulary, and her writing was always fully comprehensible to the reader, the overall organization required support. In order to make a coordinated effort to support Galyna, Ms. Perez shared with her colleagues that she was working on increasing Galyna's oral participation, lowering her affective filter, motivating her to read more with a range of high-interest reading materials, and implementing several targeted scaffolding strategies, such as sentence starters, paragraph frames, and outlines, to help her maintain focus on her topic.

→ STOP AND REFLECT ←
What were Galyna's greatest assets as a new arrival to the United States? How would you support her through the trauma she has experienced? What would you do to help her further expand her language and literacy skills?

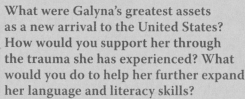

Mateo

Mateo came from Mexico to the United States first when he was twelve years old. He arrived with his mother, who was sponsored to take on a housekeeping job in an up-and-coming suburban community in Texas. She found her job very demanding, and after six months she had no choice but send Mateo back to live with his dad in their hometown in central Mexico. When Mateo rejoined his father and the rest of the family, his life had shifted, and he found himself taking care of a lot of adult responsibilities when he just wanted to be a kid. He also didn't quite fit in with his peers anymore—they saw him as too American. A couple of years later, tragedy struck, and his father passed away unexpectedly. Mateo came back to the United States to reunite with his mother, bringing along two of his siblings. Much of his life, Mateo has been helping out, fixing things around the house and the neighborhood, earning some money with odd jobs, learning how to balance working and going to school at the same time, and even partially shouldering the family's financial responsibilities.

Mateo is now sixteen, is in tenth grade, and continues to juggle his life: he spends half a day in a regular high school classroom earning credits toward his high school diploma. Then he catches a school bus to ride over to the local career and technical education center, where he participates in the automotive and small engine maintenance and repair program in the afternoon. He enjoys his CTE classes, where he learns about parts of the engine, the difference between two-stroke and four-stroke engine theory, and how to be safe around machinery—which seems to be emphasized a lot! But he is most looking forward to the hands-on learning at the garage every other day, where he can work together with his classmates on all the donated cars. Three or four times a week, he joins his mother's second cousin to help with his landscaping business. His family expects a lot of him, but he has high hopes for himself, too. He is dreaming about having (and carefully saving money for) his own car one day.

In his regular high school classes, he appreciates his teachers very much, but he is working up the courage to tell them that he does not want books in Spanish anymore—or, rather, he does not want books in Spanish only. He would prefer to get materials—both readings and assignments—in Spanish *and* English. He finds that this side-by-side approach really works for him. He can check what he needs clarification on in a Spanish document, but he wants to challenge himself to do as much work as possible in English.

→ STOP AND REFLECT ←
What are Mateo's strongest assets as a learner? What experiences or student characteristics can his teachers tap into? How would you recommend Mateo should advocate for himself?

Look Beyond the Label

Developing level students are in a unique position. They have reached high levels of competence with everyday communicative skills; have mastered some essential academic language and can use it when collaborating with classmates; can decode and comprehend high-interest, low-readability texts, especially when working with peers; and get by quite well using a range of helpful phrases and expressions and expressing themselves with more fluency. As adolescent multilingual learners, they might feel self-conscious of their accents, of always looking for the right words, of trying to figure out who they are as they are developing a new identity in a new language and in a new place. With strategic scaffolding, visual support, and background knowledge about academic content, they can access and gain a solid understanding of what is presented in class, participate actively in authentic topic explorations, and maintain interest in challenging content. When it comes to expressing themselves orally or in writing, they use words, phrases, and short sentences with some hesitation but increasing confidence; they have yet to develop independent facility with more complex academic language and literacy skills, hence the name *developing*. Holly Sawyer, National Board Certified secondary ESL specialist, challenges her developing students to build a tower using only twenty sheets of paper. This fun activity incorporates listening, speaking, and problem-solving skills as students negotiate the task, reflect on what works and what does not, and redo the task until they succeed (see Figure 3–1).

An important reminder: as indicated in the previous chapters, be prepared for your students to be at slightly different English language proficiency levels in each of the four key language domains. Some of your students might achieve the developing level in oracy (speaking and listening) but not in literacy skills (reading and writing), whereas others may reach or surpass this level in their interpretive language skills (listening and reading) but not yet in their expressive (speaking and writing) skills. They are going to be effectively relying on visual representations and demonstrating understanding. As suggested before, always consider strategies presented across

Figure 3–1 Joyful Learning and Celebrating Success Are Essential to Language Development and Community Building

Other Labels for Developing Level		
TESOL	**Hill and Miller (2014)**	**WIDA**
Developing	Speech emergence	Developing

ELPA (2016)	**New York**	**California**	**Texas**
Progressing	Transitioning	Expanding	Intermediate

Figure 3–2

the five proficiency levels in this book instead of strictly referring to this chapter alone when you work with developing level secondary students.

As you can see in Figure 3–2, the developing level of language proficiency has many other labels, depending on the theoretical framework you refer to, the state or country you live in, or the language development standards you use.

Consider What the Research Says

The zone of proximal development provides an oft-cited framework for understanding the role scaffolding may play in language acquisition (Vygotsky 1978). According to Vygotsky's original definition, the ZPD "is the distance between the actual developmental level as determined by independent problem solving and the level of potential development as determined through problem solving under guidance or in collaboration with more capable peers" (86). The concept of ZPD is well suited for all stages of language development, including the unique context in which developing level secondary MLs are situated: they often have to figure out language use under the guidance of, or in collaboration with, others—peers, classmates, friends, coaches, and educators. And as adolescents, they tend to seek out their peers rather than adults, so let's keep that in mind when planning supports for these students.

There is a growing body of research exploring the ways MLs may be supported to develop independence and agency, and among them is scaffolding. Coe and colleagues (2020) beautifully capture the essence of scaffolding when they suggest that it "provides a gentler entry, but the destination remains the same" (32). This way you

Figure 3–3 A Developing Level Student Successfully Tackles a Complex Task with Scaffolds

don't compromise the rigor and high expectations, and you help build students' confidence, self-esteem, and autonomy as they rise to the challenges you set for them and show you what they can do. For example, graphic organizers and scaffolded outlines support student independence in Kelly Cray's ELD classroom (see Figure 3–3).

An important distinction has been made between *macroscaffolding* and *microscaffolding. Macroscaffolding* refers to a carefully planned, more comprehensive approach to integrating content and language instruction across a unit of study, including attention to sequencing lessons aligned to overarching unit goals, and *microscaffolding* is the lesson-by-lesson, immediate, readily available support you offer learners (Daniels and Westerlund 2022). Both are critical: consider how the arc of your lessons gradually builds conceptual understanding and discipline-specific skills while at the same time building language and literacy. On the other hand, short-term planning or in-the-moment adjustments to your lessons will bring about a much-needed boost to student participation. In short: provide *access* and *engagement*—every lesson, every day!

Based on Aída Walqui's (2006) early work, the field of education has shifted away (or, perhaps to be more accurate, *is in the process of* shifting away) from watering down the content, reducing tasks to bare bones for MLs, or oversimplifying the language we use in class. Instead, "teaching subject matter content to English learners requires amplifying and enriching the linguistic and extralinguistic context, so that students do not get just one opportunity to come to terms with the concepts involved, but in fact may construct their understanding on the basis of multiple clues and perspectives encountered in a variety of class activities" (169). Research on scaffolding continues to expand. Two important takeaways from our current understanding are (1) we should offer the amount and type of support students need (*if* they need it), and (2) we should later remove the support from the teaching and learning experience when it is no longer necessary to ensure student independence. See Figure 3–4 for an example of a writing scaffold created by Ashley Garry, secondary ELL teacher. She adjusts the level and amount of support provided in this tool based on her students' readiness to tackle the task.

Text-Analysis Paragraph
(Conflict / Theme)

In literature, a *conflict* is a literary device characterized by a *struggle* between two opposing forces.

Conflict provides crucial tension in any story and is used to drive the narrative forward.

Topic Sentence: _____ (title) teaches readers that _____ (central idea).
Introduce: In the story, the author discusses this idea when _____ (context)
Cite: The author writes, "_____ (evidence)" (page).
Explain: This example of _____ (literary device) reveals that _____ (explain).
Relate: Therefore, the author demonstrates _____ (restate central idea).

Figure 3–4 We Must Adjust Scaffolded Tools Based on Students' Needs

Understand Developing Level Secondary Multilingual Learners

Although there is no set definition of what *developing* means, by and large, your MLs at this level will successfully participate in everyday communicative activities and will be able to converse, read, and write about a range of academic topics in English using appropriate vocabulary and grammatical structures. Let's look at what expectations you can have for developing level students or, as aptly put by WIDA (2020), what these students *can do.*

When it comes to *listening,* you can expect your students at the developing level to successfully participate in large-group or small-group activities within the following parameters:

→ follow a series of simple instructions

→ follow directions with multiple steps

→ organize information that is visually supported

→ capture key ideas from oral presentations

→ stay engaged in classroom discussions that have a central focus, pretaught vocabulary, and topic familiarity for MLs

→ follow along with teacher or student presentations that have ample visual support

Regarding *speaking* skills, you will find it most rewarding to watch as your developing level students become more comfortable with English and do the following:

→ participate in everyday conversations and basic academic dialogues

→ use vocabulary needed for everyday communication with increasing confidence

→ express ideas with emerging academic vocabulary (though at times they will be looking for precise words and substituting them)

→ use simple sentences indicating more and more complex ideas

→ begin to try more extended sentence structures, though errors are common and expected in pronunciation, word choice, sentence structure, and grammar

→ respond to questions or prompts with progressively more detail, stringing two or more sentences together

→ become more fluent in conversation

→ retell events in sequence

→ describe people, places, actions, and familiar as well as novel ideas

- → negotiate with their peers in familiar social and academic contexts
- → begin to self-monitor and self-correct

When it comes to *reading,* students at the developing level are expected to show a range of skills that expand with focused instruction and sustained opportunities for practice. They can

- → decode familiar text with increasing fluency
- → read and comprehend *key* ideas in accessible resources
- → demonstrate understanding of what they have read by using visual and text-based representations
- → identify main ideas and key supporting details in narrative and expository texts
- → distinguish text features
- → use context clues to figure out the meaning of words
- → rely on grade level resources that offer visual or context clues (such as anchor charts, word lists, word boxes, and graphic organizers)

Finally, in the area of *writing,* your developing level students will gain new milestones as they begin to do the following:

- → describe people and places using increasingly varied vocabulary in simple sentences
- → accurately use some content-specific vocabulary
- → produce narratives using longer (and increasingly more complex) sentences
- → compare and contrast ideas, people, and places
- → produce short expository writing with more and more detail
- → take notes of what is presented orally or through digital recordings that they view or listen to
- → annotate reading selections with more detail
- → use more complex sentence frames or sentence starters by adding their own ideas and words

Middle school ESL teacher Elizabeth Choi implements reading and writing workshops with her students. She reads a range of age- and grade-appropriate texts aligned to the core standards with them. She generates deep discussions about the topics they're exploring to prepare them for independent writing. See Figure 3–5 for an example of how she captures her students' ideas about ostriches protecting themselves and then uses color coding to sort, categorize, and name the patterns that emerge from students' responses.

See Figure 3–6 for the essay a developing level student wrote after receiving the multistep scaffolding Elizabeth Choi offered to the class.

Consider your expectations for your developing level students and how they are able to show whether they understand what they hear or read and how they are able to express themselves orally and in writing. My expectation for Galyna is that she will get social-emotional support from the entire faculty trained in trauma-responsive education. At the same time, she'll begin to develop more fluency in speaking and writing. As her teacher, I would encourage her to rediscover her love of reading and would ensure that she could respond to grade level materials with carefully designed scaffolds in place, including lots of digital resources to get her motivated and engaged (see more ideas on engagement later in this chapter).

As a student at the developing level, Mateo will be participating in challenging academic learning tasks as well as the technical assignments he'll be exposed to in

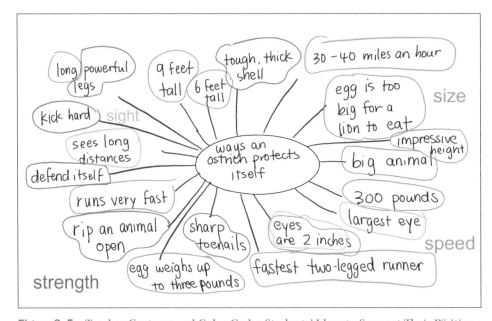

Figure 3–5   Teacher Captures and Color Codes Students' Ideas to Support Their Writing

How Ostriches Protect Themselves

An ostrich protects itself from predators with its size, strength, and speed. First, an ostrich protects itself with its size. For example, an ostrich egg weighs 3 pounds, also an ostrich can be 9 feet tall. Second, an ostrich protects itself with its strength. For example, an ostrich has powerful legs and can kick hard and enough that can kill a lion. Also, an ostrich has sharp toenails and a thick shell. Finally an ostrich protects itself with its speed. For example, an ostrich is the fastest two-legged runner so it is difficult to catch becuase of its size, strength, and speed it can protect itself from predators. In conclusion, ostriches protect themselves with their size, strength, and speed.

Figure 3–6 Student Essay About How Ostriches Protect Themselves

his CTE program. I would fully affirm his desire to tackle new material in English first while also validating the practice of using resources available both in English and in Spanish that he discovered for himself. I would challenge him to form study groups that could meet during the afternoons when he is not working in his family's landscaping business to prepare for the rigorous automotive certification exams.

Begin Here with Developing Level Students

Although the preceding broad-brush descriptions will help you understand what your secondary MLs can do, the challenge is to create learning activities that not only target and meet students where they are but appropriately challenge them to advance their proficiency as well. You can best support students at the developing level through helping them expand their vocabulary, engaging them in academic conversations through sentence level supports, and applying a range of additional scaffolding techniques and adaptations of grade-appropriate texts, assignments, and activities that push their thinking and invite them to use language with increasing complexity.

When you welcome a student at the developing level in your class or when emerging students move to this next stage, be prepared to (1) integrate vocabulary building across content areas and contexts, (2) offer differentiated sentence frames and sentence starters to enhance students' language participation, and (3) adapt texts and assignments to make grade level material accessible and to support students' academic discourse.

Integrate Vocabulary Building Across Content Areas and Contexts

Although some vocabulary acquisition strategies may apply to both MLs and their English-speaking peers, others more specifically target MLs. In their now-classic work, Beck, McKeown, and Kucan (2013) suggest a concise, three-step approach that involves a "thoughtful introduction to a set of words, interesting interactions with the words, and assessments of students' knowledge of the words" (364). These three steps appear to be well aligned to the needs of developing level students since they have an expressed need to build their vocabulary in a coherent way to enhance comprehension and their participation in academic tasks. However, when adapted to the context of working with developing level MLs, the three steps look slightly different:

1. Prepare student-friendly explanations for the words that make sense to teach your MLs considering their prior knowledge and experience with the concepts. All the definitions or explanations must include words the students are already familiar with to avoid any further confusion. Photographs, pictures, sketches, drawings, realia (real-life objects), short video clips, diagrams, or any other visual support should accompany the words when you introduce them, but make sure they are more supplementary in nature.

2. Engage students in a range of meaningful activities that allow them to see, hear, and use the words in a variety of ways and in a variety of contexts, including lots of conversation and joint meaning making. (See the tips on page 88 for specific ideas.) Because students at this level already have a large amount of tier one vocabulary (everyday words such as *home* and *happy*),

it's time to build tier two vocabulary (high-frequency academic words such as *duty* and *summarize*) and tier three vocabulary (discipline-specific words such as *acute* and *obtuse*). MLs learn new words when they have multiple meaningful encounters with the target words in different sentences and contexts and where the words appear with each other. Remember that understanding academic language does not happen by being able to define isolated words: instead, your students need time as they make sense of the concepts, use the words independently, and apply them to new situations over multiple days.

3. Use formative assessments to gauge students' understanding as well as productive use of the target language. The self-assessment tool in Figure 3–7 allows students to preassess a set of words the unit will require. For a self-assessment of this nature, make sure you carefully select words that are important for the unit, so students can both reflect on what they know and use the assessment task for language development. To borrow a metaphor from exercise science, one way to accelerate learning for MLs and build academic language power is to intentionally integrate multiple domains and stack learning tasks. For example, the students self-assess, activate prior knowledge, coconstruct meaning, and learn new vocabulary when they work in pairs with a self-assessment word-sort task such as the one in Figure 3–7.

Self-Assessment Word Sort		
Words We Have Heard Before	**Words We Have Seen in Print**	**Words We Can Use on Our Own**

Figure 3–7

Consider these tips, transferred to practice from current research (see, for example, Baker et al. 2014 and Helman, Dennis, and Kern 2022) and applied to the secondary classroom:

→ **Target no more than five or six words per lesson for direct instruction.** Why? The brain does not hold on to long lists of words; instead, a carefully selected group of words presented in context and with lots of supports will go a long way!

→ **Follow the three-step protocol over several days.** Why? One-shot deals don't yield retention for vocabulary learning. Language acquisition is like a dance—you take lots of steps in many directions.

→ **Use multiple modalities for vocabulary acquisition.** Make sure students hear the words; see them in print and digital texts and in partially completed note-taking pages; and write the words, too, through authentic activities. Why? Students need multiple meaningful encounters with words in order for them to stick.

→ **Make it functional—focus on phrases and language chunks instead of isolated words.** Why? Word lists are de-contextualized. When you teach words that go together and form phrases and meaningful language chunks, students are more likely to use and internalize them while they also develop fluency of expression.

→ **Teach students how to use linguistic clues and context clues by looking inside words (word parts and cognates) and outside the words.** Why? These strategies help students become more independent and more linguistically oriented language learners.

→ **Use technology to enhance vocabulary learning.** Why? There are an increasing number of technological tools and numerous apps available to introduce, practice, and review words and even to self-assess.

Learning words and phrases will be much more valuable for MLs if you connect the learning to a whole range of other language and literacy learning opportunities and authentic engagement with others. Secondary MLs are knowledgeable about so many things in the world, and they are savvy about how languages work universally.

Ofelia García and Cristian Solorza (2021) remind us that "meaningful language can only be produced freely, creatively, imaginatively and generatively by an author whose 'I voice' reflects their own subjectivity" (516). In my experience as a multilingual learner and teacher, I've found that words stick so much better if they are

→ *essential* (I need to use them),

→ *personally relevant* (I choose to use them),

→ *contextualized* (I understand the situation in which to use them), and

→ *applicable to multiple situations for multiple purposes* (I can determine how to use them).

In Sarah Elia's secondary ELL classroom, students regularly review key concepts to better prepare for midterm and final exams. For example, when they were reviewing enduring issues in global studies, she had them play a word game. One student was given a term but could not see what it was. The classmates shared all the information that they could use to describe the term, including events in history that were relevant to the word, and the student tried to guess their word. When the student identified the word, they rotated roles, and another student tried to guess a new word. (See Figure 3–8.)

Offer Differentiated Sentence Frames and Sentence Starters

One frequently used strategy to enhance oral communication as well as written responses among MLs is offering language supports. The best ways to scaffold MLs' developing language use may be providing models, teacher and peer examples, or *partial* models. A sentence starter is just as its name suggests, the first few words of a sentence that give your students

Figure 3–8 Gamelike Activities Are Highly Motivating. Photo Credit: Adile Jones Photography

a partial model for constructing more complete oral or written utterances. A sentence frame often contains the first few words as well as other structural features, such as a verb or an additional noun or adjective phrase, often placed later in the sentence. Based on your students' varied needs, you can decide how many of these language frames you will make available and to whom.

Keep these points in mind regarding the goals for this type of support:

→ The students will do the actual talking (not just repeat sentences).

→ The students will talk more than before (to develop confidence and be fully engaged in the conversation both cognitively and emotionally).

→ The students will talk while authentically interacting with each other (to discuss increasingly complex core content concepts using increasingly complex language).

Some MLs at or beyond the developing level may find sentence frames limiting rather than supportive since they wish to put their ideas in their own words. Always encourage that! A scaffold is there if and when needed but not to force students into a uniform script or to stifle their curiosity about language or their desire to experiment with expression.

Figure 3–9 shows a table tent cocreated by Shanna Meyer, a high school math department chair and instructional coach, and Pamela Schwallier, an EL program director, to support math talk in high school classrooms.

Adapt Texts and Assignments

With increased text complexity, developing level MLs may often find themselves overwhelmed with the density of the texts. There are several choices and approaches you can try to ensure they, too, have access to the grade level curriculum at the instructional (or perhaps even at the independent) level rather than at the frustration

Figure 3–9 Table Tent with Math Sentences

level. Regardless of the grade level or content area you teach, think of all the ways that you can make a reading selection more meaningful and accessible by *scaffolding up*. Consider the following list of suggestions for reducing the linguistic load but *not* the academic challenge for MLs:

→ graphic representations—pictures, diagrams, photographs, student- or teacher-created illustrations

→ explanations of *power words*—bilingual, monolingual, or pictorial glossaries

→ outlines with essential information provided and open space available for student notes, illustrations, or reflections

→ summary charts and tables that serve as reference guides or group study tools

→ highlighted text that emphasizes main ideas and key details

Each member of Ha's family chose to leave something behind. What do these objects tell us about that character? *(What do the objects symbolize?)*

1. **Choose a character and an object they "Left Behind"** in the poem on page 57.

2. Include:
   - A focus statement (answers the question/prompt)
   - Use quotes (2–3)
   - Explanation: Show how the quote/their decision represents their character and what is important to them.
   - Conclusion

_____ left behind _____ and this tells us that _____
_____

In the poem "Left Behind" in stanza ____ it states _____
"_____". This means
_____.

Then, in stanza ____ the poem says "_____
_____".

This detail tells us that _____
_____.

In conclusion, _____
_____.

National Board Certified, secondary multilingual specialist, and EL and ELA teacher Laura Griffith uses a quickwrite quiz based on *Inside Out and Back Again* (Lai 2013) to support her students (see Figure 3–10). She colorcodes the directions and matches each step to the scaffolded paragraph frame.

Figure 3–10 Assessment Tasks Also Need to Be Scaffolded for MLs

Focus on Multidimensional Strategies

Following is a selection of multidimensional instructional practices and strategies for supporting developing level students, organized into four main strands: (1) social-emotional support; (2) experiential learning support; (3) support across multiple modes of communication (including supporting visual literacy, building oracy, and building literacy); and (4) technology integration. Keep in mind that you can use many of these strategies with all levels of language proficiency, so as you read through the book, try to avoid limiting your strategy use to the designated language proficiency level where the strategy is first introduced.

Social–Emotional Support for Adolescent MLs

Developing level adolescent learners' well-being and academic engagement depend on a number of factors, of which you must already be mindful (no pun intended). Researchers have documented what you and I have witnessed when working with adolescents: there seems to be a gradual but predictable decline in engagement from the end of elementary school through about tenth grade. A team of researchers at OECD (2018) identified some important indicators specifically focusing on immigrant youth that we need to carefully consider and proactively address:

→ students' sense of belonging at school;

→ their satisfaction with life in general;

→ their level of school-related anxiety; and

→ their motivation to achieve.

When students have high levels of motivation, when they have a sense of belonging, and when they understand how much adults care about them, they find a way to show it. Kathy Lobo, secondary ESL teacher, is like you and so many educators working with MLs—she cherishes her students' notes, messages, cards, and other expressions of appreciation. Figure 3–11 shows a card Kathy recently received from one of her middle schoolers, who moved back to Japan.

Figure 3–11   A Heartfelt Thank-You Card

Have you ever seen any of your adolescent MLs becoming disengaged from the learning process temporarily or for a longer period of time? Have you tried to understand possible causes and search for viable responses? By using the following set of questions and selecting from the tips below each, you can get closer to understanding what might be going on and plan strategically to address these issues.

→ **Do they understand what is being said and taught?**

- Implement multimodal, multilingual, multilevel scaffolding.
- Check for understanding frequently.
- Encourage peer-to peer learning (students might just learn more from each other than from you).
- Use various models of lesson delivery and infuse technology tools to enhance comprehension.
- Teach about and encourage self-advocacy when students need help.

→ **Do they have ample opportunities for authentic meaning making?**

- Give students choices in their in-class activities and out-of-class assignments.
- Illustrate the usefulness and practical utility of what you are teaching.
- Encourage mistakes and help students to accept them as part of the natural process of learning anything.

→ **Does limited prior knowledge about certain topics interfere with processing?**

- Begin each unit with an irresistible hook.
- Continue your unit of study with a shared exploration of what everyone needs to know.
- Personalize aspects of the unit to better align to students' interests.
- Flip your class by preteaching and front-loading essential background information (see more about flipped learning later in the chapter).

→ Do they make meaningful connections to their own lives and lived experiences?

- Learn about your students so you can help make those connections for them and with them.

- Learn about your students' countries of origin and cultural heritages.

- Learn a few phrases and sentences in your students' primary languages (let them be the teachers and you the striving learner, trying hard to remember words and pronounce sounds correctly).

→ Integrate your students' out-of-school lives and literacies (including digital and nontraditional kinds of knowing) into the curriculum.

How would you determine your role in all this? How can you embrace a powerful stance as an educator of adolescent MLs? Borrowing from Lisa Delpit's (2013) seminal work, let's all collectively agree to be *warm demanders*, who "expect a great deal of their students, convince them of their own brilliance, and help them to reach their potential in a disciplined and structured environment" (77). The challenge—and amazing opportunity—you might be facing with this student group is to create a learning environment in which your students become and remain highly motivated and engaged to learn, an environment where they know and celebrate their own brilliance rather than get weighed down by perceived deficiencies. Can we collectively commit to that?

It is up to us to create vibrant learning spaces for adolescent MLs filled with peer interactions; project-based, hands-on, and kinesthetic learning; integration of visual tools and technology; recognition of what they already know; and so on. As Morrison and colleagues (2020) remind us, "non-threatening, nurturing environments fulfilling students' cognitive, linguistic, and socioemotional needs contribute to higher academic achievement and motivation to learn science among bilingual students" (257).

Not just in science, but in all subject matters!

Not just learning content, but growing as self-reliant, self-determined, independent young adults!

Not just achieving academically, but developing confidence to self-advocate, to take risks without fear of ridicule or embarrassment, and to manage their in- and out-of-school interactions and relationships!

Secondary ESL teacher Johanna Amaro uses realia to make her classroom come alive. Students learn and use new vocabulary from their project-based units by identifying and utilizing the items labeled on the table (see Figure 3–12). Students learn the meanings of words and practice them when creating their projects.

Experiential Learning Support

All students benefit from hands-on learning that invites them to get to know a topic through experiments or explorations or by creating or building something collaboratively. The more authentic a task, the more likely students will use language to collaborate and make sense of the task. Project-based learning (PBL) is well suited for developing MLs, and (like many other strategies and approaches discussed in this book) it will also be beneficial for your students in multilevel classes. In fact, heterogenous grouping for PBL is highly recommended to maximize opportunities for academic socialization, interdependence, and peer learning.

Design experiential or project-based learning opportunities

Based on your local context, experiential learning opportunities and project-based learning may be supplemental to your teaching or may be central to instruction in

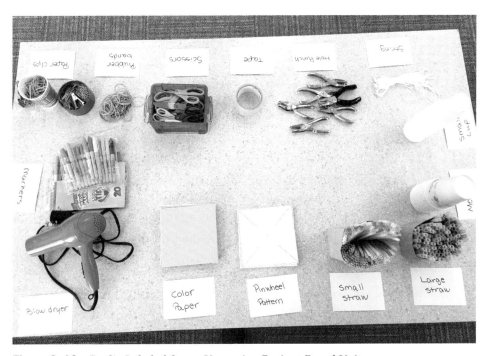

Figure 3–12   Realia Labeled for an Upcoming Project-Based Unit

your classroom or school. I agree with Lauren Ayer (2019), who suggests four key steps to take for successful projects:

1. Plan with the end in mind.
2. Assist students in developing their own questions.
3. Encourage students to think like experts.
4. Make sure the projects are presented or published for an authentic audience.

Think of the project or experiential activity as a complex vehicle for academic language and literacy development alongside discovery learning tied to content goals. With this in mind, I recommend you create three key conditions to help MLs be successful with experiential or project-based learning:

1. Before you begin, analyze the content demand and the linguistic demand of the project you are planning for MLs. Ask yourself these questions:
   - What kind of background knowledge or contextual understanding is required for the project?
   - Are there any prerequisite content or linguistic skills my MLs need to work on before beginning the project?
   - What are some specific academic language features and language experiences (on the word, sentence, or discourse dimension) needed for the project?

2. Create collaborative work groups that ensure active participation by all learners, including MLs.
   - Maximize collaboration and interaction by strategically placing MLs in heterogeneous groups with English-proficient peers as well as other MLs who share a primary language.
   - Plan projects that give MLs opportunities to effectively use their home language and literacy skills.

3. Scaffold MLs' participation in one or more of the four key language uses (WIDA 2021) and consider how to engage them in all four ways of communicating about their projects. Think about what language supports MLs will need to:

- *inform* their peers about the project and negotiate all aspects of the group work;
- *explain* the purpose and the outcomes of the work the students have engaged in;
- *argue* a perspective they had to take during or as a result of the project; and
- *narrate* the key steps they took or the essential components of the project.

See Figure 3–13 for an example of a chemistry project from Nathan Townsend's high school classroom. Hands-on learning opportunities like these support students in developing their content knowledge and language as well as their creativity.

Prepare students for successful presentations

A project becomes more meaningful to students when they present it or share it with a real audience. After reviewing what a good presentation looks and sounds

Figure 3–13 A Developing Student's Final Chemistry Project

like, you can share live or digitally recorded model presentations to analyze and critique. Students will benefit from cocreating a rubric or checklist of the qualities an effective presentation should have. Have teams of students plan and rehearse their presentations before delivering them in person or virtually. A planning guide like the one in Figure 3–14 can further assist students at the developing level in ensuring clarity, structuring their presentation, and determining roles and responsibilities.

Support Across Multiple Modes of Communication

Developing level adolescent multilingual learners may feel that they have come so far with English, yet they will also recognize that proficiency is still a long way away. They need to keep up their stamina and engage in learning in the secondary classroom, where rigor is increasing rapidly and demonstrating their knowledge and understanding in English might continue to be difficult.

Supporting visual literacy

We can select instructional tools that aid students in learning new content and skills and in building their academic language. Although you can continue to use the visual supports discussed in Chapters 1 and 2, aim for a subtle shift for developing level

---

Group Project Presentation Planning Guide

Group members: _____

Our presentation is about _____.

Our audience is _____.

Our audience will (know, feel, or do) _____

_____.

Student A will _____.

Student B will _____.

Student C will _____.

To make our presentation engaging, we will open with _____

_____.

To make our presentation engaging, we will end with _____

_____.

Figure 3–14   Group Project Presentation Planning Guide

MLs to allow the visuals to serve as supplementary resources rather than as the main vehicle of communication. See Figure 3–15 for some suggestions on how to do this.

Building oracy

Developing level students will especially benefit from frequent, structured, and purposeful opportunities to interact with their peers and teachers to build their expressive and academic language skills as well as encourage risk taking. Here are some concrete ways to build student confidence:

→ Start with partnership building, allowing students to choose with whom they wish to partner.

→ Introduce the triad structure (discussed in Chapter 2) to help them negotiate multiple perspectives and practice active listening and turn taking.

Tips for Using Visual Support with Developing Level Students	
Types of Visual Support	**Tips**
Show a three- to five-minute video to preview or review the material.	Use Screen-Cast-O-Matic to create your own videos and try flipped learning (see more about flipped learning later in this chapter).
Create one-page summaries that synthesize all the key information needed for the lesson.	Have an advanced ML or English-proficient peer create summary charts to synthesize a unit or chapter for extra points or service-learning credit.
Create partially completed graphic organizers with key ideas already inserted.	Use the one-page summary you or your students created and remove some information from it. If needed, add a word or phrase box to offer additional scaffolding.
Generate anchor charts with visuals.	Co-create charts and graphs with your students so they can participate in the process of capturing and illustrating information. (See Figure 3.16 for an anchor chart that helps students in secondary EAL teacher Alycia Owen's room understand key ideas.)
Continue to encourage visual representations created by your students.	Invite students to add increasingly detailed descriptions and explanations with their visual representations. Encourage students to talk and write first before they visually enhance their thinking

Figure 3–15

- → Move to flexible grouping strategies that are at times heterogenous and at other times homogenous.
- → Vary the partnerships you initiate for MLs, ensuring that they frequently interact with a variety of students for different academic purposes.
- → Set up group work with clearly assigned roles for accountability purposes.
- → Invite MLs to share about their own lived experiences and showcase their in- and out-of-school expertise.
- → Engage students in collaborative tasks with shared responsibility, such as cocreating summaries and outlines or preparing small-group presentations.

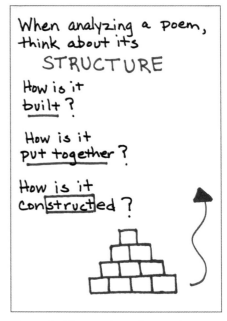

Figure 3–16 Anchor Chart to Support a Literacy Task

When multilingual learner specialist Victoria Seelinger's students were learning about directions, they played an interactive directional game (much like the popular game Battleship) in which they had to deduce each other's location (see Figure 3–17). Students said they thought it was cool, and they enjoyed the game's structure.

Building literacy: Supporting reading development

Since developing level students will rely heavily on context clues and thrive when working with familiar topics and with other students, reading supports for MLs must consider these learner characteristics. When you differentiate reading selections for MLs, make sure your students are both challenged and engaged. Whenever possible, let students choose what they read. Donalyn Miller and Teri Lesesne (2022) explain, "Reading self-efficacy and joyful reading identities develop from lots of opportunities to choose reading material based on one's own interests and needs" (78). If students are unsure about how to choose a book, provide guidance. For example, they might look for new titles from a beloved author, explore a particular topic of interest, get recommendations from peers, listen to book talks, or sample the text (Miller and Lesesne 2022). Providing choice and access to a range of high-interest print-based and digital texts is a powerful motivator for young readers. The key at this stage is to boost comprehension and to develop a healthy reader identity. Sarah Elia (ENL teacher) and Meghan Keyser (ELA teacher) have collaborated to offer their students project-based choices to respond to literature, as shown in the following box. See Figures 3–18 and 3–19 for some student responses to these options.

Figure 3–17   Students Learn Through an Interactive Game

Building background knowledge

One continued challenge developing level students face is when the readings are not connected to their prior knowledge of the topic or to their personal experiences. To proactively address this, plan on situating all reading instruction in *assessing, activating*, and *building* background first, then *connecting* it with new learning. (This is a slightly modified ABC of background knowledge with two *A*s: AABC). Review Figure 3–20 for a collection of commonly used strategies for each of the three phases of working with student background knowledge. While this list can be helpful, it is by no means comprehensive. Feel free to brainstorm with your colleagues and add even more strategies.

Project Option One: Diary or Scrapbook

Choose a character from the novel. Describe their thoughts or perspectives about events. You may use drawings you create, pictures you cut from magazines, small objects, or photos you copy and paste. For each page or slide, you will need a diary entry explaining and analyzing what is happening during that current event. The diary or scrapbook must have seven to ten entries that span the time period in the book. This could be a virtual scrapbook or a physical scrapbook.

Project Option Two: Illustrations

Illustrate five buildings from the novel. For each drawing, write at least one paragraph describing the building, its residents, and what it would have been like to live there. Each paragraph should have one quote from the book that supports your drawing of the house.

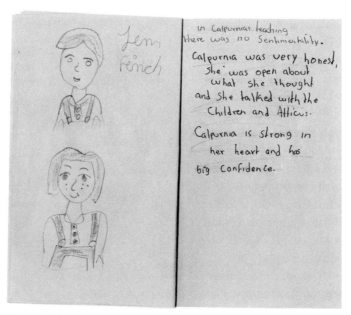

Figure 3–18 Student-Created Scrapbook About Calpurnia in *To Kill a Mockingbird*

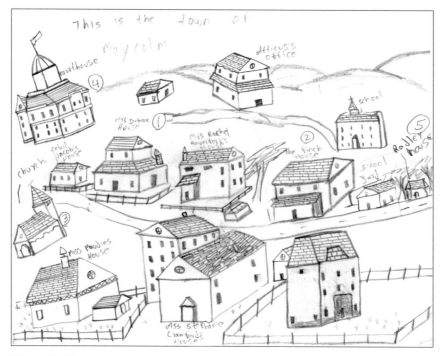

Figure 3–19 Student-Created Location Illustrations for *To Kill a Mockingbird*

Background Knowledge Is Key for Reading Success

What Is Your Aim?	How Will This Help Students?	Possible Lessons/ Activities
Assess background knowledge	Assessing background knowledge enables you to understand what students actually know and can already do related to the topic. (Don't assume.)	• free writes/quick writes • brainstorming • sketch-it • anticipatory guides • questionnaires • think tanks
Activate background knowledge	Activating background knowledge brings information and skills needed for new learning to the forefront.	• brainstorming • personal stories and connections • curricular connections • mind maps • video clips • web searches
Build background knowledge	Building background knowledge bridges gaps identified through engagement with the first two phases.	• real-life experiences • field trips • virtual tours • guest speakers • background reading and viewing activities • hands-on learning • research experiences
Connect background to new learning	Making connections is what the multilingual brain does—constantly linking the known and integrated skills to new learning.	• learning Logs • KWL • KWHL • journaling

Figure 3–20

Doing guided exploration to support reading across text sets In addition to continuously assessing, activating, and building their background, it would be highly beneficial for you to do some guided topic exploration (reminiscent of guided reading) that's specially adapted for secondary students. If you have never used or heard of guided reading before, it is typically implemented as a small-group instructional approach in elementary literacy classrooms with a strategic use of before-reading, during-reading, and after-reading activities and differentiated reading materials matching students' reading levels. Timothy Shanahan (2018), renowned reading expert, encourages an adaptation of guided reading for adolescents with an emphasis on (1) reading the same text(s) with teacher guidance and through peer interaction and (2) amplifying access to complex material through scaffolding and shared interpretations of what the text says. As a next step, try to combine literary or disciplinary text sets that gradually increase text complexity, so you can guide your students to higher levels of comprehension. Among many others, experienced high school teacher Kristi Moore (2021) observed that "employing guided reading requires an instructional spiral, moving students gradually to longer and more complex or nuanced texts," which is exactly what developing level MLs need. Consider the following tips for guided topic exploration with your secondary MLs:

→ *Carefully select shorter texts or excerpts that either are on the same theme (taking your readers on a journey across genres) or are in the same genre (helping them develop a deeper understanding of the text type).* Why? Guided reading with adolescents works best if you complete the shared exploration of the selection in one class period.

→ *Make sure the sequence of texts gradually builds understanding and incrementally increases text complexity and cognitive challenge.* Why? This type of lesson planning is well grounded in the gradual release of responsibility model (see, for example, Frey, Fisher, and Almarode 2023).

→ *Set the stage for reading with anticipation guides or other background-building reading activities.* Why? Cold reading for MLs at this stage will continue to be challenging (revisit ideas for background building earlier in this chapter).

→ *Model multiple reading comprehension strategies and invite students to employ them to make meaning of the text, to summarize what they are reading, and to make connections among readings.* Why? MLs need opportunities to develop their comprehension, their critical thinking skills, and their independence with increasingly complex yet manageable texts.

→ *Incorporate stop-and-process times for small-group discussions about the text.* Why? Chunking or breaking down tasks and texts retains the rigor of the work while allowing students to seek help from others as needed in their language of choice, interact with the text and each other, and take a much-needed brain break from processing in English.

Alycia Owen, secondary EAL specialist, created the infographic in Figure 3–21 about using intentional grouping configurations and designing meaningful interactions.

Reading for joy and abundance
Reading for joy and abundance sounds quite poetic because it is! It's also essential to strong reading skills. Donalyn Miller and Teri Lesesne (2022) write, "If reading volume and variety are the keys to reading achievement success, what conditions engage kids to read widely and in volume? Lots of joyful, independent, relevant reading" (28).

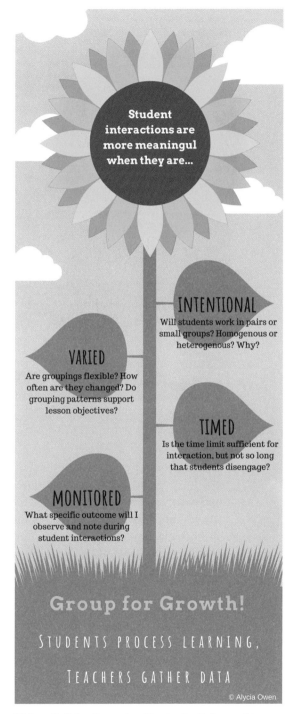

Figure 3–21 Grouping Strategies Infographic

Figure 3–22 **Student Reading with Enjoyment**

When your secondary MLs reach for books (or read print or online magazines or other digital materials), they begin to develop a reader identity in English. They need access to lots of reading materials that interest them, so remember to get to know your students, especially what their out-of-school passions or future aspirations are.

You have to show them that you are a reader and you fully embrace your reader identity. Read aloud to the students an excerpt from what you are currently reading and aim for sharing across genres and sources: fiction, poetry, scientific discovery, and news items. As you read each time, share one metacognitive or metalinguistic behavior (more on that in Chapter 4): marvel at a word choice, pose a question, point out something that is confusing or puzzling to you, invite comments from your students. To acknowledge your adolescent learners' need for peer interaction, encourage or implement study groups, reading clubs, inquiry circles, and so on for shared reading experiences. To honor your adolescent learners' need for autonomy, offer lots of choices and make those choices available both physically in your classroom and digitally online. Secondary ELN teacher Amanda Haleiko's students appreciate that they can choose where and how they wish to read (see Figure 3–22).

Building Literacy: Supporting writing development

Writing instruction for developing level MLs is often conceived as an important bridge between oral language development (oracy) and literacy (Heron et al. 2023; Soto 2014). How can your MLs write something that they have never uttered? Ensuring ample prewriting activities that allow for exposure to rich oral language and provide opportunities for MLs to begin to express themselves in more complex ways is critical to writing growth. Oracy and literacy are intertwined for MLs, and so are the skills they already have in their home or primary language and in English. Modeling writing is a complex endeavor for MLs to follow. There are at least four ways you can employ modeling in the context of writing instruction:

1. **Task modeling:** Explain the expectations and break down the writing task or writing prompt to ensure clarity.

2. **Process modeling:** Show the steps of the writing process to your students or reveal the process you applied to a piece of your own writing.

3. **Product modeling:** Show what the final product may look like so your MLs see the big picture and can better visualize what they will be working on.

4. **Linguistic modeling:** Make explicit connections between how the spoken words you use carry meaning (this is what we say) and how you transfer them to a written piece (this is how we write it down), and offer ample language models.

See Figure 3–23 for an example of process and linguistic modeling. Notice how middle school EAL and language support specialist Jane Russell Valezy shows the process of writing an email to more effectively communicate with teachers on the left and offers a linguistic model on the right.

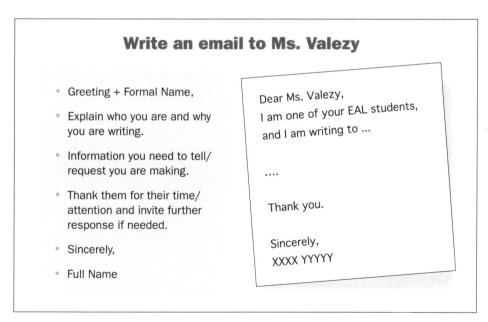

Write an email to Ms. Valezy

- Greeting + Formal Name,

- Explain who you are and why you are writing.

- Information you need to tell/ request you are making.

- Thank them for their time/ attention and invite further response if needed.

- Sincerely,

- Full Name

Dear Ms. Valezy,
I am one of your EAL students, and I am writing to …

….

Thank you.

Sincerely,
XXXX YYYYY

Figure 3–23 Modeling How to Write an Email to a Teacher

You can help your students at the developing level move beyond their earlier accomplishments of crafting simple sentences and short paragraphs when they were at the starting and emerging levels in several ways:

→ Make writing a daily practice through journaling, where you continue to encourage home language responses alongside English as well as illustrations.

→ Keep a dialogue journal, in which you maintain a written dialogue with your students and respond to them in writing. (You can also have students keep peer-to-peer dialogue journals.)

→ Use quickwrites (entry tickets or exit tickets, reflection prompts) as pathways to enhance fluency.

→ Set up writing partners or writing teams that allow students to brainstorm ideas, outline first drafts, and participate in shared-writing activities. (If a developing level student orally describes a character in the story or recounts the key events, their partner or team member may capture these ideas and write them down in more cohesive language.)

→ Engage them in structured, modeled prewriting activities that activate and build prior knowledge, vocabulary, and expressive language chunks about the topic of your upcoming lesson.

→ Guide and support them through the writing process, with attention to audience and purpose.

→ Provide peer-editing and shared-writing experiences.

→ Value your students' cultural experiences, inviting them to write about what they know and what they sincerely care about using the language(s) of their choice.

→ Embrace the translanguaging *corriente*, or multilingual language flow, in which students use all their languages authentically (García, Johnson, and Seltzer 2017).

→ Offer writing scaffolds: partially completed graphic organizers, note-taking pages, sentence frames, and paragraph and essay outlines.

Figure 3–24 shows how grade eight English teacher Gina Zlake models introduction and conclusion paragraphs for her students as they prepare to write a text-to-film comparison essay.

Introduction

Hook
(introduce the
book title, year,
and basic plot)

Thesis
(How does the
movie director
create a different
experience
than the book
author?)

How the Grinch Stole Christmas is a classic holiday
story, written by Dr. Seuss in 1957. It tells the story of
the Grinch, an isolated, grouchy outsider who hates
everything Whoville stands for: Christmas, community
spirit, and love. He "steals" Christmas by ruining the
Who's presents and holiday displays, only to discover
that the Whos continue without them. Through this
experience, the Grinch learns that Christmas is about
love and not gifts and ultimately becomes part of the
group. In 2000, director Ron Howard adapted this story
as a live action holiday blockbuster, but he made choices
that created a different experience for the viewer. In the
film, Howard makes choices that make the mood more
humorous and deepen the Grinch as a character. These
choices make the viewer sympathize with the Grinch in
a way that does not apply to the book, and, an invented
character, Augustus Maywho, emerges as the true villain
of the story.

**Background
info.**
(introduce the
movie director,
year, and general
major changes)

Conclusion

**Restate
the thesis.**
(use different
words)

**Synthesize
your major
ideas.**
(don't just list
them)

Howard's film not only brought the Grinch to life, it also
made changes that enable viewers to give him another
chance. While Howard stayed true to Seuss's basic theme,
he took creative liberties with the story's mood and the
Grinch's childhood. These changes encourage viewers to
sympathize with Grinch, a reaction that is never inspired
in the book. Additionally, Howard created the character
of Augustus Maywho who becomes the true villain of the
story for his lifelong bullying of the Grinch. In fact, by
the end of the movie, the Grinch actually becomes a hero.
**Howard's live version of How The Grinch Stole Christmas
took a creative spin on a beloved holiday story, and may
one day achieve a classic status of its own.**

End with
a thought-
provoking
statement.

Figure 3–24 Color-Coded Models
for Paragraph Construction

Technology Integration

Can your students stop you whenever they want to or need to?

Can they pause the lesson when they need more time to process?

Can they ask you to start the whole lesson over and repeat everything you have just taught?

Can they rewind you or fast-forward you?

Actually, they can . . . and if you have ever tried or heard of flipped learning, you know where I am going with these questions. Flipped learning is a powerful approach for providing your developing level MLs (and others that need it) early access to the content that you are planning to teach during an upcoming lesson. The Flipped Learning Network (2014) explains, "Flipped Learning is a pedagogical approach in which direct instruction moves from the group learning space to the individual learning space, and the resulting group space is transformed into a dynamic, interactive learning environment where the educator guides the students as they apply concepts and engage creatively in subject matter."

In short, flipped learning gives your students the ability to familiarize themselves with content at their own pace while freeing up your class time for learning that is more student-centered, creative, and collaborative for MLs.

There are certainly some challenges with any technology-based innovative approach, but the benefits have been well documented. For over a decade, Helaine Marshall (2019) has advocated for flipped learning as a way to create fertile spaces for multilingual learners. When Avary Carhill-Poza (2019) studied flipped learning implemented with MLs in urban high schools, she found that flipped learning helped offer "personaliz[ed] classroom instruction to the point that each student's needs and strengths could be taken into account. The availability of text, video, and audio afforded students multiple entry points to course content" (98).

Notice When Developing Level Students Are Ready to Move On

Although most schools determine levels of language proficiency and student placement based on annual standardized assessments such as ACCESS by WIDA, ELPA21, and NYSESLAT, formative assessments and progress monitoring play an important role in your day-to-day work with MLs. To track the progress that students at the developing level make, take a multidimensional approach. Your data collection should include teacher observations of oral language skills (listening and speaking), student

How Can You Flip Learning?

1. **Find or create a video.** You might look for videos on a well-known platform such as Khan Academy, Discovery Education, the History Channel, or PBS. You'll need to carefully evaluate videos you find online to ensure that they explain the content accurately and that they are interesting and accessible to students.

   Or you might record your own video using Screencastify or ScreenPal, Zoom, or some other digital tool.

2. **Design a viewing task.** What will students do or look for as they watch the video? The viewing task prepares students for the upcoming in-class lesson, which will integrate peer interactions, explorations, and whole-class and small-group discussions. Here are a few examples of potential viewing tasks your students can complete:

   - Take notes on the video using a structured (partially completed) note catcher.
   - Answer questions you posed about the video in a Google doc.
   - Prepare questions to ask their peers or you when back in class the next day.
   - Come better prepared to discuss the topic in class.

3. **Ensure that students have the tools they need.** If students do not have devices at home, make arrangements so that they can use the school library computers or may take a tablet, laptop, or iPad home.

4. **Before the lesson, have students watch the video and complete the task.** Remind students that as they watch, they have the option to

   - put on subtitles in English or in a language of their choice if needed;
   - choose when they want to pause the video to have extra time to process it; and
   - rewind or rewatch it as needed.

work samples to document how their writing skills are developing, and reading conferences where you can check on their comprehension and also monitor how their reading skills are growing and to what degree they are able to use reading strategies. An important and often underutilized dimension of understanding where students are and where they are heading is inviting students to self-assess and to set goals.

You will start noticing that developing level students are bridging over to the next language proficiency level when they can follow multistep directions with ease and participate in more complex academic conversations in small-group or whole-class settings. They will also use more complex sentence structures that include more precise academic vocabulary and varied word choice. You will notice how their metalinguistic awareness is developing and they are gaining independence. I would expect Galyna to understand and summarize the key ideas in grade level material and, with scaffolds and support, to discuss what she reads and hears with increasing detail. I would expect Mateo to navigate grade level materials and technical manuals and resources in his CTE program with increased success as well as begin to write increasingly more complex sentences and paragraphs. Both students will begin to demonstrate more independence as a language and literacy learner, though quite differently because of the difference in age and learning contexts. With guidance and support, both can learn to accurately self-assess their developing language and literacy skills and to set their own goals.

Chapter Four

Supporting

EXPANDING

Level Multilingual Learners

Meet *Expanding* Level Secondary Multilingual Learners

Let's meet Janaína and Sandley, two students who are at the expanding level of English language acquisition. They come from different backgrounds and attend school at different grade levels, but they have both achieved some important linguistic milestones and have developed an extensive range of skills when communicating in both writing and speaking in English.

While reading about their in- and out-of-school experiences, keep in mind the cultural, linguistic, and academic assets they bring to their classes, schools, and larger communities. If you have encountered students with similar backgrounds, how do these stories compare with the ones you know? What experiences and characteristics do these children share and what is unique about their language and literacy progression? The goal of this chapter is to support expanding MLs' academic, linguistic, and literacy development beyond the developing level.

> If you want to build high, you must dig deep.
>
> —MONGOLIAN PROVERB

Janaína

Janaína is a fourteen-year-old ninth grader. Her parents brought her and her little sister, Mariana, from Brazil to a small apartment in the United States when Janaína was in sixth grade. They already had extended family members settled nearby, so there were many cousins and friends who helped them acclimate. Both sisters had some prior exposure to English and strong writing and reading skills in Portuguese. In their new schools, the sisters were assigned to different classes in different grades, and both demonstrated steady progress in English, though the two girls could not have been more different from each other. Now, a few years after the move to the United States, Janaína's teachers often refer to her as a sponge, which both annoys and puzzles her. Unlike her sister, who really enjoys books, and often curls up with a new novel to read by herself, Janaína does not like reading for enjoyment and seeks out after-school clubs, sports teams, and other activities where she can socialize with her peers.

When it comes to reading, Janaína gets frustrated when she comes across unfamiliar words or phrases, so she simply skips over them. She discovered that she can *fast read* (the term she uses to describe what is essentially skimming and scanning). She is confident she still gets the gist of everything she is reading and everything the teacher is presenting in class. She prefers fast-paced music videos, action movies on Netflix, or just about anything that pops into her YouTube feed to her textbooks or required readings. Each time her teachers offer a choice to submit assignments in alternate formats, she makes videos, makes Google slide decks with a voice-over, or even dabbles in Prezis.

Janaína knows her sister keeps a stack of personal dictionaries at home, and she often takes a quick peak inside Mariana's latest notebook, but she does not like to write things out or look words up in a dictionary. Everybody says she seems to just pick up the language. Janaína's outgoing personality not only helps her with making new friends but with her in-class participation, too. She seems to be ready to contribute to whole-class or small-group discussions without much hesitation even when she has not yet fully formulated her ideas.

→ STOP AND REFLECT ←

What personality features and learning strategies help Janaína make steady progress? In what ways can her teachers further capitalize on her strengths and support her with her academic development?

Sandley

Sandley first came to the United States when they were in first grade in the wake of the devastating earthquakes in Haiti in 2010. Tragedy struck, and the family lost Sandley's two older siblings, as well as their home, their business, and just about everything except their hope. They came to the United States and stayed with extended family members and friends on Long Island, in New York City, then in New Jersey, and then back on Long Island. It seemed that every few months they had to pack up and move to stay in a new place. Sandley's parents decided to return to Haiti after fifteen months of trying to get back on their feet in the United States, only to return to New Jersey for Sandley to join third grade at the end of the school year. It was all very confusing and painful; Sandley did not really understand why their family did not live in the same place long enough for them to make friends. As expected of most Haitian children, Sandley has always been obedient of their elders and especially respectful of their teachers. While they developed some foundational English skills, their primary language used at home continued to be Creole. Since eighth grade, Sandley had been hovering at the developing and expanding levels, making slower than anticipated progress in English and still remembering how tough fourth grade was: Sandley was learning to read in English while the rest of the class was reading chapter books and engaged in deep conversations. Sandley knew they were different from the rest of the class and having to leave the classroom for pullout services for years during the elementary grades made them self-conscious. Middle school was even more challenging. Sandley continued to feel guilty about being the only surviving child in the family, coupled with the fact that they did not know anyone to talk to about their gender identity. They felt it was safest to stay quiet in class, sit in the back of the classroom, and not try to call any attention to themselves. As they began high school, they accidentally discovered comic books and became a huge Deadpool fan. In tenth grade, a new guidance counselor joined their school, and he took his time to get to know the students and establish a new club called GSA (which stands for Gender and Sexuality Alliance). The tenth-grade ELA and social studies classes also had a lab period added with the ELD specialist supporting students, so Sandley started to come to their classes a bit better prepared. To their great surprise, the ELA teacher had a graphic novel version of the very first assigned reading, *To Kill a Mockingbird* (Lee 2018), and the social studies teacher frequently used comics as well as a wordless graphic novel (*Nat Turner*, by Kyle Baker [2008]) to introduce topics they were learning about in class.

> → STOP AND REFLECT ←
> How does Sandley cope with the many challenges they seem to have to face? What type of further academic, linguistic, and social-emotional support could they benefit from?

Look Beyond the Label

The term *expanding* suggests that students are in a much fuller command of understanding English, broadening their language and literacy skills, widening their linguistic repertoires, and participating in new and increasingly challenging language experiences every day. The word *expand* comes from the Latin *expandere*, which means "to spread out." If you have previous experience following the development of multilingual learners across multiple years, you must have marveled at how they begin to spread their wings, ready to soar . . . yet they might just continue to glide by. Elise White Diaz, secondary language coach, not only reads a range of genres with her students but also invites them to try writing a range of genres. See Figure 4–1 for a sample page of a graphic novel by one of Elise's students.

So, a word of caution is in order: although you might have observed a student's steady, relatively fast language development from the starting to the emerging level of language proficiency, you might notice that their rate of language acquisition may not be as fast now as it was at previous levels. Not only do the complexities of academic language and the linguistic demand of academic tasks begin to catch up with the students, but you might also notice that some of them seem to be slowing down with their language and literacy growth, some might even hit a plateau, and others might even be now labeled as *long-term ELLs* or *LTELLs* or, as a recent publication suggests, *experienced multilingual learners*, to use a more assets-based term (Huynh and Skelton 2023).

The expanding level can be a very sensitive time for many adolescent learners, especially those who stay at this level for long. They might feel comfortable with their communicative competence yet are self-conscious about not being able to move to the next level of proficiency with ease. In *How We Learn*, Stanislas Dehaene (2021) presents some important discoveries in the field of cognitive neuroscience and reminds us to consider both the emotional and cogni-

Figure 4–1 Student-Created Graphic Novel

tive dimensions of the brain *and* the emotional and cognitive dimensions of the learning environment we are creating for our students: "Negative emotions crush our brain's learning potential, whereas providing the brain with a fear-free environment may reopen the gates of neuronal plasticity" (xxiii). Adolescent MLs require robust instruction with the right amount and type of structures and supports, safe learning environments, and carefully designed opportunities for nurturing their autonomy as they move forward with their language development. Lindsey Fairweather, secondary EAL teacher, connects core content learning to language development opportunities such as combining science with creative writing. Here's an example of a challenge she created for her students:

> *Imagine you wake up and you have been shrunk! Suddenly you find yourself stuck inside a cell. Choose whether it's a plant cell or an animal cell and tell us what you see and feel!*

One of Lindsey's expanding level students seemed to have had a blast producing their text (shown in the box below).

Today I'm telling you about the day I got stuck inside a cell, so, I was there relaxing on my couch when suddenly . . . I shrank. I shrank A LOT. I couldn't see anything right then I looked up and saw a brown looking thingie. So I continued advancing. I didnt need to walk, there was a jelly like substance helping me float through the place. I was getting more and more confused about where I actually was. So I saw a bunch of red things, I didn't know what they were either, then I realised. Jelly like substance? Shrinking? Brown looking thing? Red things . . . ?

I was inside a cell. I knew I was. I was still confused about how that happened but there was no time for questions, I had to get out, and as quickly as possible. Then I started "swimming" through the cytoplasm . . . I swam, swam, swam . . . then I finally got to where I needed! I could see the cell membrane . . . ! But . . . something wasn't right . . . there was something behind the cell membrane, a thick yellow thing. Oh no. Was I trapped inside a plant cell?

I needed to escape as quickly as possible, but I knew the cell wall would block my path. So just to confirm my doubts, I looked down and I saw floating along with the red things: green things too. Yeah. I was inside a plant cell. So I decided to plan an escape from there, but I didn't know what to do. If I tried to escape through the cell membrane I would be stopped by the cell wall. So I started to think about where I really was. A cell membrane has the place where the mitochondria and chloroplasts float, a nucleus on the top left side of it, and . . . One large vacuole. Okay so I finally knew I was probably stuck inside the vacuole and I had to find a way out. Wait . . . I know how to get out!

(continues)

(*continued*)

Then I remembered I had my scissors in my pocket when I was sleeping and they probably shrank too! So I searched my pocket and there it was, my scissors. So I know what to do. I started cutting through the vacuole to see if I can get out and I managed it. But now, I was on the chloroplasts' and mitochondria's way. I didn't know what happened if you got hit by either but I wasn't going to stick around to see. So I quickly swam to the edge and away from their path. Then I started making my attempt, I tried to cut through the cell membrane and cell wall, and guess what? I did it!

Suddenly, I woke up, sweat was all over my face and I was hyperventilating.

Then I realised, it was all a bad dream. I was so happy but so bad at the same time. So I just went back to sleeping hoping I wouldn't return to this dream. It was all a dream.

Other Labels for Expanding Level		
TESOL	**Hill and Miller (2014)**	**WIDA**
Expanding	Intermediate fluency	Expanding

ELPA (2016)	**New York**	**California**	**Texas**
Proficient	Expanding	Expanding	Advanced

Figure 4–2

As you can see in Figure 4–2, the expanding level of language proficiency has other labels, depending on the theoretical framework you refer to, the state or country you live in, or the language development standards you use.

Consider What the Research Says

A growing body of research addresses learner agency, learning strategy instruction, and student autonomy, with some very promising work in this field focusing especially on MLs. *Agency* is defined as a person's ability to take an active role in determining what their life path will be; on the other hand, *autonomy* refers to one's ability to develop independence and respond to challenges by applying the knowledge and skills they have to new situations. Agency and autonomy are two critical characteristics we should pay attention to, considering research findings as well MLs' complex needs in a postpandemic era (Honigsfeld et al. 2022). When students have the opportunity to develop metacognitive awareness (thinking about their own thinking), their agency is fostered (Ferlazzo and Sypnieski 2022). Autonomy is also evidenced when students understand how they develop new skills and how they can transfer those skills to address new challenges they face.

The importance of strategy instruction is well supported by decades of research by Oxford (2017), who also notes that "deepening strategy instruction to make it more personally valuable for autonomy could be transformative for learners" (2). More recently, Nina Parrish (2022)—among many others—has been advocating for metacognitive strategy instruction. Guiding all students, especially expanding level adolescent MLs, to become more self-directed and self-reflective learners will contribute to their success in and outside your classroom, and developing strong metacognition is one key pathway to achieve that.

Figure 4–3 Nurturing Student Agency and Independence Is Critical for Expanding Level Students

While we want to foster independence and nurture self-regulation, peer interactions remain necessary for MLs' continued language acquisition and social-emotional development. Keep in mind that expanding level adolescent MLs (as well as their peers on all other proficiency levels) benefit from both cognitive models of learning that focus on critical reasoning, problem solving, experiments, and metacognition as well as social models of learning that embrace collaborative practices, discussions, and debates. In Figure 4–3 a ninth-grade student carefully completes a science experiment before discussing her findings with her peers.

Understand Expanding Level Secondary Multilingual Learners

MLs who are recognized to be at the expanding level of language proficiency represent a range of language and literacy skills across the four domains. Language acquisition continues to be fluid and dynamic, so expect your MLs to demonstrate different levels of skills and competence in listening, speaking, reading, and writing.

Expanding level students are increasingly able to read complex texts for information, to express their ideas in writing and speaking in more precise ways, and to maintain personal and academic conversations by asking clarifying questions, building on their peers' contributions, and explaining their own thinking.

With an assets-based—rather than deficiencies-oriented—philosophy in mind, let's look at what positive expectations you can have for expanding level students or, as aptly put by WIDA (2020), what these students *can do*.

When it comes to *listening*, you can expect enhanced evidence of comprehending English by these students. They are likely able to

→ understand main ideas and most supporting details

→ understand directions (but will continue to benefit from visual supports and repetition)

→ understand and respond to both everyday and academic conversations

→ process digital recordings (both audio and video) with increased confidence

→ comprehend moderately demanding, contextualized oral presentations

Regarding *speaking* skills, you will notice that MLs at the expanding level will

→ participate in formal and informal conversations with increased confidence and clarity

→ speak comfortably about familiar and academic topics in small- or large-group settings

→ communicate more fluently and spontaneously (though some hesitation, self-correction, or rephrasing may be observed)

→ use an expanding repertoire of grammatical structures

→ make phonological, syntactic, or semantic errors that do not interfere with the overall meaning of the communication

→ utilize a variety of words and idiomatic expressions to offer detail about the topic

When it comes to *reading,* your students will demonstrate more complex skills as they begin to

→ read and understand texts on familiar as well as novel topics with relative speed and fluency

→ read for enjoyment and academic purposes across genres with increased stamina

→ comprehend all main ideas and most supporting details in more complex academic texts

→ glean new information by reading texts with clear organization and illustrations (but they may struggle with dense texts that are written in a more technical language on unfamiliar topics)

→ figure out meanings of most words using context clues and prior knowledge (see Figure 4–4 for an anchor chart codeveloped by Alycia Owen, secondary EAL specialist, and her students)

→ continue to find idiomatic expressions and words with multiple meanings challenging

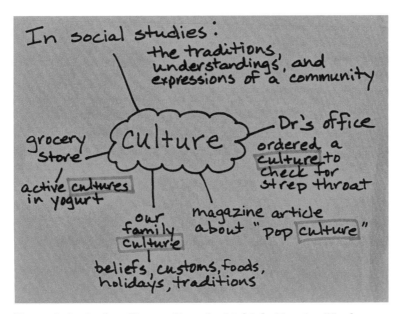

Figure 4–4   Anchor Chart to Unpack a Multiple-Meaning Word

As far as *writing* is concerned, these students can

> → effectively communicate ideas related to familiar topics (both everyday and academic)
>
> → write for personal and academic purposes with increasing focus and clarity
>
> → demonstrate solid control over simple sentence structures
>
> → experiment with increasingly more complex grammatical structures (but they may produce some nonstandard sentences)
>
> → take notes with increasing accuracy and detail based on information they read or listen to
>
> → write in all major grade-appropriate academic genres (narrative, expository, persuasive), although a lack of discipline-specific vocabulary or complex sentence structures may be occasionally evident
>
> → organize ideas into logical, well-developed text (with scaffolds and support), with occasional errors in word choice or grammar

Students at the expanding level demonstrate noticeable independence in all four language domains as well as with their academic, content-specific literacy skills. This growth helps them handle the complex linguistic expectations they encounter in a variety of academic settings. Janaína, for example, can more easily make sense of texts using various linguistic and technological resources that she learned to harness. She can confidently engage in everyday and academic conversations with her classmates, and her writing reflects effective use of sentence structures and paragraph organization with occasional errors that do not distract from understanding her message. Sandley finds independent research projects a pathway to success. They devour graphic novel adaptations of the classic and contemporary literature. Sandley reads and writes about grade-appropriate topics, which are often presented to them in digital formats. They still tend to withdraw to the back of the class and rarely participate in whole-class conversations, whereas in small groups and especially in pairs, they are becoming more comfortable with the interaction and confident with the language.

Begin Here with Expanding Level Students

MLs at the expanding level require experiences that allow them to venture into challenging academic learning with confidence and take risks to express themselves both in writing and in speaking with voice and agency.

When you have expanding level students in your class, your priority must be to help them become self-directed, independent learners while recognizing that "the observational reality is that second language learners at higher levels of English language proficiency require *more* time to master linguistic features than lower level language learners" (Cook et al. 2008, 8). In addition, MLs at this level are working on much finer points of language than they were at earlier stages, so they need to rely on a coach *or* learn how to coach themselves. Three practices that support expanding level students are (1) raising metacognitive awareness of their learning process through strategy instruction, (2) building metalinguistic skills, and (3) offering one-on-one coaching support. Sarah Elia, secondary ENL teacher, attends to all these needs through complex learning opportunities. For example, students in her global history class might do a gallery walk, examining excerpts that were pulled from the state regents exam essay section. Each document is similar in theme (in this case, industry). Students first use a sticky note to guess the time period of the document or image, then they annotate the documents by describing what they see (see Figure 4–5). On the final gallery walk, they identify one to two enduring issues that might be related to each document and choose one enduring issue to focus on that they will ultimately analyze in their essay.

Figure 4–5 During a Gallery Walk, Students Identify Enduring Issues. Photo Credit: Adile Jones Photography

Raise Students' Metacognitive Awareness of Their Learning Process

Learners of all ages can develop effective strategies that aid in their social and academic language use as well as continued academic language development (Oxford 2017). When you show your students how you self-monitor and self-assess your own language and literacy use, you model these linguistic and literacy behaviors while also fostering metacognitive awareness in students. Remember, you want them to be able to monitor how they use the language, process complex academic content, check their own written work, or reflect on their learning to develop more independence and to set attainable goals. The following three main questions, originating from Fisher, Frey, and Hattie's (2021) work, provide a plausible place for students to start reflecting on their own learning. The questions I have added will extend or deepen the reflection process:

→ **What am I learning?**
- What are the goals and objectives of the unit, lesson, or task?
- How can I articulate those goals in my own words?

→ **Why am I learning this?**
- How is it relevant to me, my current needs, or my future goals?
- How can I connect what I am learning in school to the real world?

→ **How will I know that I have learned it?**
- How can I self-assess and find gaps in my own learning?
- How can I show others what I have learned?
- How can I seek and receive feedback from others, such as my peers and teachers?

See Figure 4–6 for an example of creating an overview and setting clear goals and expectations for a unit from an eighth-grade class cotaught by Jane Russell Valezy (middle school EAL and language support specialist) and David Gardner (social studies teacher).

Metacognitive strategies

There are numerous guidebooks and research articles dedicated to the topic of strategy instruction in the context of metacognition. Let's look at a few actionable steps that I have found to be especially helpful for adolescent MLs.

First, I recommend students get a planner and use it. When students begin a new academic year, they often get a planner from the school. If not, a simple academic calendar or a notebook will do! Invite your students to decorate their planners with their favorite things, including what they are planning or hoping for their lives—thus they can turn their planners into vision boards. Ask them: "What goes in that planner? What goes on the outside of the planner? Are you going to use it?"

Next, help students become goal setters. Each course, each unit of study, and each project will have subject- or even topic-specific requirements. Take time to review them with your students and help map out a pathway to completion. It's important to get all MLs engaged in goal setting and planning early on in the academic year.

Students should also practice tracking and monitoring their progress. Model for students how they can take an active role

Figure 4–6 Unit Overview

in their progress by asking themselves questions such as these: "What do I know and what else do I need to learn? What resources and strategies have I used that help and what does not? In which classes am I understanding the material well? In which classes do I need to seek additional resources or opportunities for practice?" In her seventh-grade science classroom, Tami Cutter applies the approaches to learning (ATL) domain and regularly invites her students to reflect on how they engage in the learning process to ensure that her students become self-directed, successful independent learners (see Figure 4–7).

Reflection Form for Self-Monitoring				
SELF-MONITORING	**Always**	**Frequently**	**Sometimes**	**Rarely/ Never**
• I am responsible and respectful in class.				
• I use class time wisely. (on time, focus on classwork, take notes, work efficiently)				
• I monitor my own progress and seek help when needed.				
• I am a creative problem solver and I challenge myself to do my BEST.				
Self-Monitoring OVERALL				
I do a good job of . . .				
I need to work on . . .				

Figure 4–7

You can also encourage them to choose a tool to be a better time manager or project organizer. Secondary school schedules can be overwhelming for all students but especially for MLs who might not have experienced the type of multitasking required of students in U.S. schools. Identify digital tools the students are already using to manage their time and assignments or introduce some new ones.

Lastly, help them become critical thinkers and inner evaluators. Encourage students to pause and reflect on what they already know about a topic or task and have them compare how this new learning is different from what they have already encountered or mastered in the past. Similarly, ask students to think about what strategies have they tried that worked (or did not work so well) in the past. Alycia Owen, secondary EAL specialist, has found that the quickwrite format takes little time. She also likes to add metacognitive prompts as part of other activities. For example, after a review activity in class, she might include an exit ticket, like these:

> *At home, what is your most effective way to review for a quiz?*

> *Turn to a partner and share: In your experience, what is the best environment for studying?*

You might be thinking, *But how do I find the time for all this when I must cover the curriculum, differentiate instruction for students with academic, linguistic, and access needs, and assess and grade dozens of assignments every week?* I hear you! Yet, pause for a moment and think about the powerful position you are in to teach your multilingual learners "how to optimize their use of study time to promote efficient and effective learning and better retention of knowledge and skills in both generic learning to learn lessons or within their subject-specific classes" (Surma et al. 2022, 2). In the end, you will enhance the effectiveness and efficiency of your lessons when you also focus on metacognition and study strategies. Claudia Leon, middle school ENL teacher, uses peer editing as an approach to enhance

Peer Reviewer's name: _____ Author's name: _____			
EVIDENCE BASED WRITING - peer editing			
	Yes?	No?	If YES, provide evidence. If NO, provide suggestions to improve the writing.
Did the author **RESTATE & ANSWER** the question and is this the 1st sentence of the paragraph? This is also called **CLAIM**.	✓		"Anne has matured during the play and through the war because she realized what was happening."
Did the author **CITE EVIDENCE**? (provide 3 pieces of evidence that support the **CLAIM**)	✓		1) on page 21 it says "You know I think here" etc 2) on page 58 it says "every night I think back" 3) on pg. 105 "I don't care about the food."
Did the author **EXPLAIN** each piece of evidence?	✓		Yes he did
Did the author write a concluding sentence that is similar to the **CLAIM**?	✓		Yes because on the claim it talks about how she realizes what's going on.
Does ALL of the evidence have **quotation marks, slashes, page #s**?	✓		1) on page 21 2) on page 58 3) on page 108
Do all of the sentences begin with a capital letter and end with the correct punctuation (period, question mark, etc).	✓		Yes, everything has a capital letter and periods
Are there any run-on sentences? These are sentences that just go on and on and on, and have too many ideas that can confuse the reader.	✓		good job he did a good job.
Did the author include any of the suggestions that Mrs. Leon gave them?	✓		Yes.

Figure 4–8 A Completed Peer-Editing Checklist and Feedback Form

metacognition and student-to-student interaction. See Figure 4–8 for a completed peer-editing checklist and Figure 4–9 to see the students using that tool.

Study strategies

To enhance independent learning, tap into the latest findings of cognitive science and explicitly teach your expanding MLs how to make the most of their studying. Yana Weinstein, Christopher Madan, and Megan Sumeracki (2018) advocate for six specific strategies that are well documented and well supported by decades of research: spaced practice, interleaving, retrieval practice, elaboration, concrete examples, and dual coding. See Figure 4–10 for a handy explanation of what each strategy is about, how you can introduce it to MLs, and how it can be relevant to MLs.

Figure 4–9 Students Engage in Peer Editing Using a Teacher-Created Checklist

There are a lot of misconceptions among both students and teachers about which learning strategies are evidence-based and will yield the most desired results. (You might be as surprised to find as I was that summarizing, rereading, copying notes, and using keyword mnemonics are among the not-so-effective strategies.) Figure 4–11 is a metacognitive checklist for studying that can further help students integrate evidence-based learning strategies in their daily routines.

See Figure 4–12 for an example of spiraling the curriculum while also integrating language practice opportunities. The bell-ringer activities in Frank Fonseca's eighth-grade math classes frequently invite students to revisit previously learned material while also explicitly teaching or reviewing the language of mathematics.

Finally, to foster independence and to extend learning beyond the physical and time constraints of a school day, have students create their own learning tools, using both traditional materials (such as paper and pen) and digital resources. In the process of making an instructional tool, expanding level MLs will have opportunities to use their creativity and their metacognitive and metalinguistic skills. They will internalize what they are learning about while also developing independence and confidence.

Build Metalinguistic and Metacognitive Skills

You might choose to read aloud to your students from time to time and you are also likely to think aloud and share your thinking process with them across the secondary grades. Secondary MLs also need insights into your comprehension and meaning-making process when it comes to challenging texts, so make sure you also *comprehend aloud* (Zwiers 2014).

According to Zwiers, think-alouds support the development of a range of reading strategies (metalinguistic skills), whereas comprehend-alouds make visible the processing and analyzing of the language of complex texts (metacognitive skills). See Figure 4–13 for the types of sentence starters you can use to model think-alouds and comprehend-alouds with the text you are exploring with your students. Adapt these sentence starters to best fit the grade level you teach and your MLs' readiness levels.

Cognitive Strategies That Support Academic and Linguistic Development

Strategy	Simple Definitions (To explain them to your students.)	Teaching Strategies (To introduce and reinforce them in the secondary context.)	Connections (To encourage your MLs to try them.)
Spaced Practice	Don't cram, spread it out.	• Use a spiraling curriculum design. • Review previously taught material periodically. • Help students create a schedule for studying.	• "Your multilingual brain will love multiple opportunities to look at what you are studying and to practice English in new ways over and over."
Interleaving	Mix it up, leave one area of study and come back to it.	• Move around from topic to topic in your review sessions. • Use station rotations. • Shuffle some questions or problems but stay within the same general content.	• "Working your brain is similar to exercising. Think of it like an exercise or dance routine. You stay within the dance/movement but you also strengthen different parts of your practice or dance."
Retrieval Practice	Test or quiz yourself about the topic you are studying.	• Give students an opportunity to self-check their understanding and to quiz themselves or each other.	• "Try Quizlet or Chegg to test yourself. When you create your own digital flashcards, you learn and when you practice with them, you can track your progress and reflect on small improvements."
Elaboration	Ask yourself questions about the topic (and answer those questions, too).	• Encourage your students ask questions. (Ideally, they should be asking more questions than you do!) • Engage students in inquiry-based learning, student-initiated research projects, etc. Frequently use peer tutoring and small-group instructional strategies such as reciprocal teaching.	• "Learning a new language and learning something complex in that language require lots of stop-and-process times. When you pause and ask questions, you show your curiosity, you challenge yourself, and you can dig deeper into the topic."
Concrete Examples	Review examples discussed in class or found in the book.	• Apply the Gradual Release of Responsibility model to model task examples and to engage in shared explorations.	• "I know you like to see the big picture first and then closely examine what a particular task or assignment looks like when it is completed. Go back to those examples when you study."
Dual Coding	Look for visual and text-based resources on the same topic.	• Make all your teaching multimodal. Invite students into meaning-making through visual and textual examples.	• "You've heard the old saying, 'A picture is worth a thousand words,' right? Well, think of having that picture in front of you and the words that explain the picture, too! It is the best of both worlds!"

Figure 4–10

Study Strategy Checklist

Name: _____ Date: _____

What I am studying: _____

	Most of the Time	Some of the Time	Not Yet
In general, I have a goal in mind before I begin to study.			
I plan to study difficult material over several days.			
As I study, I ask and answer questions to see how well I remember the material.			
As I study, I try to recall important details before checking them in my notes or books.			
When I study, I switch around the order of exercises or mix up the questions.			
When I study, I don't wait to the last minute to do all my work.			
When I study, I look through examples given by my teacher, discussed in class, or found in my textbook.			
When I study, I review both text-based and visual materials to better remember.			
My goals for next time:			

Figure 4–11

Good Morning!

Amelia said the table represents a nonproportional relationship with a slope of 6.

Baxter said the table represents a nonproportional relationship with a slope of 15.

x	y
2	30
8	90
14	150
20	210

Who is correct and how do you know?

Figure 4–12   A Bell-Ringer Activity in Support of a Spiraling Math Curriculum Aligned to Language Practice

Sentence Starters for Think-Alouds and Comprehend-Alouds

Think-Aloud Sentence Stems	Comprehend-Aloud Sentence Stems
Predicting	*Word or Phrase Level*
• When I read the title of this essay, I immediately thought of . . . • I predict this novel is about . . . • In the next chapter, I think the protagonist will . . .	• I noticed that the author uses the same word here . . . • I have never seen this word in the context of this topic. Let me see if I can figure out the meaning by reading ahead/looking for some examples/finding an illustration. • The author begins the sentence with the phrase . . .
Clarifying	
• I was confused when I read . . . • I had to go back to page . . . • I had to think back to what I read about . . .	*Sentence or Text Level*
Summarizing	• The author uses a very long sentence in this paragraph. Let me see how we can break it down into shorter sections, such as . . . • In this section, I noticed some sentences have a similar pattern to . . . • I noticed this section has a lot of dialogue and quotes. I wonder . . . • When I skim through the text and stop at each heading, I see the author is using a unique organization in this essay . . .
• I think this section is mainly about . . . • The most important point the author is making . . . • I think the purpose of this article is . . .	
Making Connections	
• What I just read reminds me of . . . • The section I just read is similar to . . . • When I read this section, I thought of . . . • I think the author wants me to . . .	

Figure 4–13

Adolescent expanding level students, as all other MLs, "draw on their metacognitive, metalinguistic, and metacultural awareness to develop effectiveness in language use" (WIDA 2020, 12). Let's make a commitment to nurture these skills across grade levels and content areas.

Provide One-on-One Coaching

Expanding level students may present as fluent, confident conversationalists and may also read and write close to grade level proficiency. Yet you might find that some students in this group of MLs hit a plateau or experience decelerated progress compared with their previous learning trajectory. One-on-one coaching will help students clarify their thinking and polish academic language use. Cultural and language

Figure 4–14   One-on-One Coaching Supports MLs with Targeted Interventions and Guidance

support specialist Kelly Cray regularly takes the time to confer with her students individually while the rest of the class is engaged in partner work or independent work. In Figure 4–14, Kelly is making sure her student understands the task and offering her just-in-time support.

While one-on-one conferring is highly beneficial for all students, your coaching for MLs in particular should serve a multidimensional purpose: supporting independence and autonomy—a *take charge and keep trying* attitude—as well as language and literacy development skills and concept attainment. Coaching may be scheduled regularly or may occur spontaneously to review or reinforce what the students know and do well as self-directed learners. In the past few years, the traditional ESL or ELD teacher's role has shifted significantly both in the United States and internationally (Gonzalez 2020). The ELD specialists can no longer be the sole supporters of MLs; instead, all teachers are teachers of language and literacy, and all teachers must embrace ways to empower MLs.

One way we can all advance our students' language and literacy development is by coaching them through those rough spots, offering them support through motivation, organization, and practice. Some teachers open a help desk (Dove and Honigsfeld 2018); others set up a conferring corner or conference center (Honigsfeld and Nordmeyer 2023) to create a well-established space in the classroom where seeking and receiving help are accepted. Although the name for a place for coaching support may vary from classroom to classroom, the actual practice stays similar: students either choose to or are invited to participate in short, focused coaching sessions with their teacher during designated times. When you coach expanding level MLs, take into consideration the guidelines in Figure 4–15.

Jane Russell Valezy, middle school EAL and language support specialist, invites her students to keep a learning log and track their progress at school and at home. Working with secondary students, she makes sure they can self-select practice activities that are in line with their language learning goals to encourage independence, thoughtful goal setting, and agency in their language learning. She offers a list of suggestions for how they might practice each language skill independently at home. A practice log helps with accountability if needed; it also encourages students to reflect on their learning with an open-ended section for comments or reflection. See Figure 4–16 for an excerpt from one of her students' homework practice log.

Coaching Guidelines		
Guidelines for Conferring	**How to Do That**	**What That Sounds Like**
Always use a strength-based rather than a deficit-based approach to coaching.	Build on areas that students excel at and name their strengths with precision (what the students already know and are able to do well).	"Excellent use of '_____,' our new word from today's lesson! I am looking forward to seeing or hearing you use that word again!"
Help students set periodic goals to develop independence and foster self-monitoring. (Remember to teach about the need to revisit and adjust goals as well.)	Create a weekly or biweekly plan with learning goals codeveloped with students and have them track their own progress.	"This week, let's continue working on how you use verbs in your sentences when you edit your own writing. What specific goal would you like to set for yourself and how will you keep track?"
Guide students to take responsibility for their own learning and progress.	In addition to setting goals, have students identify ways they can reach them and reflect on what they have already accomplished.	"I know your goal is to come to school prepared every day, especially having your homework done. You have done much better these past two weeks than at the beginning of the year. Can you tell me what you did differently?" "Let's go over your plan to meet your goal of having homework done every day."
Focus on study skills, organizational skills, and some other nonacademic skills that students need to overcome day-to-day in-school challenges.	Have them keep a learning log or strategy log with periodic reflections on how they tackle assignments and various learning experiences.	"Your learning log has lots of entries that talk about your study habits. I would love to see how you tackle challenging homework assignments."
Help students see themselves as expert readers and writers.	Coach them to think, read, and write like disciplinary experts do by specifically focusing on the type of academic language that is associated with each field.	"When you work on your report, remember how scientists organize their information. Do you think written notes or diagrams would help you better plan your paper?"

Figure 4–15

DATE	ACTIVITY	TIME SPENT	COMMENTS/REFLECTION
9/14	Vocabulary: Membean	10 min	The words 'Refined/Sophisticated' were interesting
9/18	Reading: Newsela	1 hr	I've tried reading it by highlighting what I don't understand exactly, and what I found interesting. It was super helpful to collect the correct information from the article.
9/18	Listening: Ted-ed video	5 min	The video was talking about why it is so hard to get out of poverty, with such reasoning, a loophole of supporting policy from the government. Also, the compelling question at the end, 'What is a power?', 'What roles should power play in a society?' impressed me a lot.
9/19	Grammar: Quill	10 min	I completed possessives and 23 questions for a placement.
9/21	Speaking: Making comments on TED I watched today	24min	The final video was my sixth recording, which means I could barely make any comments at my first trial :((. But I was satisfied with myself in the last video where I described the thought I had while watching the video the best.
9/26	Listening	10min	I listened to the podcast for the first time. It was a story about a student who developed an algorithm for diagnosing Parkinson's disease with a quantum computer.
10/5	Speaking	2 hr	I was really struggling to speak naturally but also professionally in a social study assessment video, which eventually took me more than 2 hours.

Figure 4–16   Excerpt from a Student's Homework Practice Log

Take the time to get to know your expanding level students. Conferring with your students is more private so it will allow you to provide just-right, in-the-moment scaffolds without embarrassing them in front of their peers. Embrace your role as their coach: ask lots of questions, gather information about their progress, provide choices and clear guidance, recognize their emotional state, and listen closely to their ideas. And then, remember to celebrate them, affirm what they have accomplished, and challenge them to try new things.

Focus on Multidimensional Strategies

Following is a selection of multidimensional instructional practices and strategies for supporting expanding level students, organized into four main strands: (1) social-emotional support; (2) experiential learning support; (3) support across multiple modes of communication (including supporting visual literacy, building oracy, and building literacy); and (4) technology integration. Keep in mind that you can use many of these strategies with all levels of language proficiency, so as you read through the book, try to avoid limiting your strategy use to the designated language proficiency level where the strategy is first introduced.

Social–Emotional Support for Adolescent MLs

Students who have reached the expanding level are *experienced language learners* (Huynh and Skelton 2023), yet they might not have had enough experience with self-advocacy, they might not have built up enough courage to engage in it, or they might not have been shown how or encouraged to do it. Self-advocacy may be readily connected to metacognition and metalinguistic awareness, discussed earlier in this chapter: once students know and understand themselves better as learners and as language learners, they can more clearly identify what works for them and what does not as well as articulate their requests.

So, we have to name it, model it, and practice it. Don't assume your students know what self-advocacy really is or how to engage in it: it might be inappropriate in many cultures for the students to tell a teacher directly what they need. So, first of all, define for your students that self-advocacy simply is *knowing yourself and asking for what you need*. Then take some time to explore what self-advocacy looks like, sounds like, and feels like in a learning situation, be it inside or outside the classroom or school context. To keep it manageable, let's adapt Andrew Lee's (n.d.) three-part approach to self-advocacy and teach the following four key elements explicitly:

1. Understand your strengths and needs as a multilingual learner.
2. Know what type of supports or scaffolds teachers can offer and what might help you overcome a learning challenge.
3. Communicate your needs to your teachers and others.
4. Stay focused without backing down, and repeat these steps if needed.

While these four steps seem simple, there is one more important dimension to practicing self-advocacy. According to Babette Moeller (2023), the very first step to take is to "create a classroom environment that helps students feel safe, encouraged, and empowered to advocate for themselves," which goes hand in hand with lowering the affective filter and reducing the fear of failure while learning a new language. You can teach and reinforce self-advocacy skills by using mini case studies, simulations, or role-playing scenarios related to familiar situations the students might find themselves in. For example, here's a mini case study about Jorge:

> *Jorge is a multilingual student who has a hard time keeping up with fast-paced minilessons. He understands that following the teacher's presentation without notes or visuals is going to present a challenge for him. He is going to approach his teacher and ask for written notes, outlines, or graphic organizers that summarize essential learning.*

A final word of caution here: Watch out for expanding level MLs who might also experience increasing academic anxiety and might be displaying a negative academic self-concept. They deserve a school and classroom environment where risk taking is not just accepted but valued and encouraged. Adolescent MLs are unlikely to work on expanding their language skills and competencies if they fear embarrassment or ridicule.

Experiential Learning Support

Adolescent learners are known for questioning the utility or even the meaning of what we are trying to teach them. Bryan Goodwin (2020) points out that students need to embrace two things to fully commit to learning, which have important implications for expanding level MLs' experiences in and outside the classroom:

1. This is important and interesting to me.
2. I believe I can do it (or learn it).

Your adolescent MLs can find interest, personal relevance, and empowerment when engaging in individual and collaborative inquiry-based explorations. Think of *inquiry-based learning* as an umbrella term (a very big umbrella, that is) with lots of exploratory opportunities for students to achieve many—if not all—of the following goals:

→ (re)activate student curiosity
→ develop autonomy
→ collaborate with others

→ pose questions that matter to them

→ establish learning goals based on authentic, real-life problems

→ construct new knowledge and develop new skills and dispositions

→ make mistakes and embrace mistakes by design

→ find and define their own directions while working on reaching meaningful goals

When students engage in meaningful, deep explorations focused on content area topics, their learning will be more substantial. Inquiry-based learning recognizes that students' curiosity and desire to understand drive learning; in other words, "one remarkable characteristic of inquiry is that it is done *by* the individual not *to* the individual, and this active form of learning . . . is what makes knowledge stick" (Lenters 2016, 104). Consider the following simple planning tool inspired by a more recent blog by Lee Crockett (2021), which draws on the five Cs of inquiry-based learning (curiosity, caring, connections, communication, and creation):

A Quick Planning Guide for Inquiry-Based Learning

My multilingual learners are curious about and care about _____.

They can also make connections to _____.

They will communicate their findings about _____ by creating _____.

Although you can implement inquiry-based learning with individual students, when you use it in collaborative contexts, students benefit from shared learning opportunities and interactions with each other and the material. Banchi and Bell (2008) suggest that there are four levels of inquiry, with incrementally more complex expectations for student independence. Figure 4–17 shows the four levels, their purposes, and a brief summary of what students and teachers do at each.

Based on the grade level and the complexity of the content you teach, select the type of inquiry that is most appropriate to support your students' conceptual and linguistic development. Also, keep in mind that if these levels appear a bit too constricting, feel free to embrace a more flexible, dynamic approach, "which includes moving in and out of phases to question, explore, mess around with ideas, design and redesign, try, fail, try again, and discover" (Bacak and Byker 2021, 268).

Banchi and Bell's Levels of Inquiry Support MLs				
Inquiry Type	Purpose	What Students Do	What Teachers Provide	Examples from the Classroom
Confirmation Inquiry	to introduce the inquiry process	confirm through experience what they already know	• questions • procedure • solution	explore the behaviors and density of liquids with oil and water
Structured Inquiry	to scaffold the inquiry process	generate an explanation for what they find	• questions • procedure	water plants with vinegar vs. water to create "acid-rain-like" conditions that will cause the plants to eventually die
Guided Inquiry	to provide a more open-ended process for students	design the procedure of inquiry and generate explanations	• questions	build a simple motor with a magnet, paperclips, battery, and rubber band
Open Inquiry	to give students ownership of the inquiry process	design the question and the method of inquiry as well as generate explanations	• process reminders and expectations	open-ended—students will determine all aspects of the inquiry

Adapted from Banchi and Bell (2008) and Honigsfeld (2019).

Figure 4–17

When you integrate student-driven, inquiry-based, hands-on learning opportunities in your secondary classroom, MLs' engagement and commitment to learning are likely to be reignited. To help you envision the forms this kind of learning can take, the following list names a few ways you can get started with it in your own classroom. As you look at the list, consider which of the following options would work best with your students, your schedule, and your curriculum.

→ **Place-based learning:** Students explore their *new* (or old) neighborhood's history, geography, economy, natural history, folklore, art, local traditions, and so on.

→ **Genius hour:** Students learn about and explore anything that they are interested in for a designated period (modeled after the now-famous Google 20 percent principle: employees dedicate 20 percent of their work week to an idea they are personally invested in and want to further develop rather than are assigned to do).

→ **Hands-on experimentation:** Students explore elements of the physical world with teacher guidance.

→ **Civic involvement:** Students identify a local, community-based problem that they genuinely care about and explore possible real-life solutions.

→ **Global matters:** Students choose one of the seventeen United Nations Sustainable Development Goals and study it from a personally meaningful and relevant perspective.

→ **Service learning:** Students evaluate available service-learning opportunities and select one or design more personally relevant new ones.

→ **Makerspace:** Students build something unique from materials made available to them.

→ **Games:** Students engage in designing gamelike activities for themselves or their peers using digital tools or traditional materials.

→ **Passion projects:** Students' deep-rooted interest—which may easily fall outside of the typical secondary curriculum—drives the exploration.

Figure 4–18 Exploring a Local Watershed Area

In Figure 4–18, one of high school ESL teacher Michelle Land's students explores the local watershed for benthic macroinvertebrates. The students used nets to stir up the streambed. After collecting several samples, they categorized the macroinvertebrates into three types: sensitive to pollution, mildly tolerant to some pollution, and tolerant of pollution.

They used a chart with diagrams of the different macroinvertebrates to do this. The goal was to determine if there were macroinvertebrates that were sensitive to pollution present, which would indicate the local stream had little or no pollution in it.

In case you have any doubts about the value of this type of learning or if you feel there is never enough time for it, consider how inquiry-based learning all connects back to metacognition, self-regulation, and student agency, as found by the research team at the Learning Policy Institute and Turnaround for Children (2021):

> *Well-designed inquiry learning supports the development of executive function and metacognitive skills that help students "learn to learn" throughout their lives. . . . In the course of guiding inquiry, educators can help students develop these skills through modeling of thinking, explicit strategy instruction, scaffolds for self-monitoring of thinking and actions, and regular opportunities for student self- and peer assessment. (71)*

Support Across Multiple Modes of Communication

Secondary expanding level MLs' needs for teacher support change as they become more apt at using English across the core content areas and develop metalinguistic and metacognitive expertise. But just because students present as more fluent speakers, or communicative conversationalists, or more engaged readers and writers, it does not mean we can let them manage the rest of their language development alone. This is a critical time period for students to get stuck on a plateau and not advance incrementally if we are not intentional and attentive to individual needs.

Supporting visual literacy alongside language development

While visual support is essential in earlier stages of language development, it continues to be helpful for all learners. Continue to provide multisensory experiences or multimodal input for your expanding level MLs. At this point in the students' language development, these supports are necessary to enhance cohesion and meaning making alongside (not in place of) verbal input.

Katie Beckett, a secondary ESL specialist, likes to invite her students to read descriptive paragraphs and create a drawing or a digital collage of how they see the scene in their head. After students complete their visual representations, they also answer some questions about their work to strengthen their comprehension skills. See Figure 4–19 for one student's visualization based on a paragraph of a text they read.

Figure 4–19   Student Visualization of a Setting

Graphic organizers   Instruction across all grade levels and content areas may be well supported with graphic organizers that help outline the following:

→ what the students already know—try variations of the KWL (what I know; what I wonder; what I learned) chart, such as KWHLAQ:

- What do I (already) know?
- What do I want to know?
- How will I learn it?
- What did I learn?
- How can I apply what I have learned? (Or, What action should or will I take?)
- What new questions do I have?

→ what they anticipate will happen in an upcoming lesson or target text—set up an anticipation guide or try the four Ps: preview, predict, prior knowledge, purpose

→ what concepts are developed in an upcoming unit—develop concept maps

A common recommendation is to use a small set of graphic organizers consistently to help starting or emerging MLs so they have access to complex core content or can see connections between ideas, concepts, words, and phrases, such as a well-tested set of graphic organizers including T-charts and Venn diagrams. Expanding level MLs, however, will benefit from more complex visual representations to enhance their cognitive processing skills and expressive (productive) and interpretive (receptive) language skills.

Thinking Maps®   If you are looking for a consistent or systematic way of supporting MLs' thinking, explore Thinking Maps (from Thinking Maps, Inc.). With proper training, Thinking Maps are implemented throughout whole schools to create a common visual language for teachers, students, and administrators. Each map is specific to a certain thinking process and these cognitive and metacognitive processes are concisely connected to eight visuals, each with its own protocol. Figure 4–20 summarizes the key purpose of each of the eight Thinking Maps and offers lesson ideas on how to apply them to secondary literacy and core content instruction for MLs.

Thinking Map Summary Table		
Kind of Thinking Map	Purpose	Examples from Secondary Literacy and Core Content Lessons
Circle Map	Define in context (adding a frame of reference)	• Create a frame of reference for rules within the classroom, school, or larger community. • Brainstorm about good learning habits within the context of the grade level and core content subject.
Tree Map	Classification	• Classify various organic compounds. • Summarize the achievements of the Maya Civilization.
Bubble Map	Description	• Describe the protagonist of a short story. • Describe the characteristics of primary sources in history.

Figure 4–20   Thinking Maps® is a registered trademark of Thinking Maps, Inc.

Thinking Map Summary Table

Kind of Thinking Map	Purpose	Examples from Secondary Literacy and Core Content Lessons
Double Bubble Map	Comparison and contrast	• Compare and contrast two main characters in a novel. • Compare two opposing historical rivals.
Flow Map	Sequence or order of events	• Describe the steps taken in a science experiment. • Describe the key events that led up to a significant day in history.
Multi-Flow Map	Cause and effect	• Discuss the events that led to the Declaration of Independence and the events that followed it. • Explore the causes and the effects of climate change.
Brace Map	Part-whole relationships	• Identify the major systems of the human body and the organs found in each system. • Identify all the oceans and continents. • Name parts of an insect.
Bridge Map	Analogies	• Explore the relationship between part and whole, change in size or age, or antonyms and synonyms.

Figure 4–20 *Continued*

Middle school ESL specialist Elizabeth Choi uses Thinking Maps to have her students organize their cognitive and linguistic processes. See Figure 4–21 for two examples of a Circle Map.

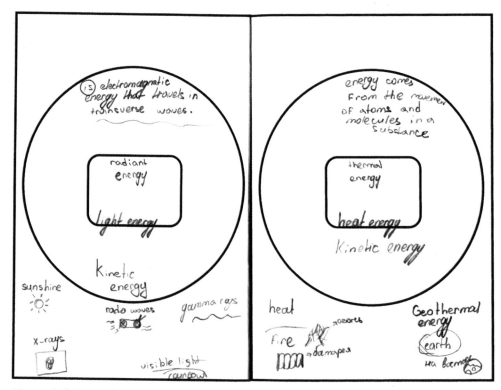

Figure 4–21 Circle Maps

Expanding oracy skills

It has been frequently cited that the classroom is the place for the much-needed "social occasions that provide opportunities for discussants to think, speak, listen, and learn together, with and across their differences, about a specified topic" (Parker 2006, 11). Let's place some much-needed emphasis on *across differences*! It is not just students at the expanding level who benefit from well-designed collaborative learning tasks; in fact, it is most effective if students engage in classroom talk across proficiency levels, languages, and cultural backgrounds. Jeff Zwiers (2019a) reminds us of the challenge of mental multitasking when we speak and listen to each other in the academic context. Students at the expanding level are past the time when the goal was to *learn to talk*; now we need to support them in well-designed, equitable opportunities to *talk to learn.* In secondary EAL specialist Alycia Owen's class, students pitch a plan: they create an informal, proposed outline for their writing, then pitch it to classmates for feedback. The students in Figure 4–22 are discussing their writing plans for expository and narrative pieces on the topic of being multilingual.

Although there are many interactive learning strategies, here I offer some specific details about two small-group instructional strategies that maintain the rigor of instruction without putting too much social pressure on MLs: intentional pairing and station rotation.

Figure 4–22 Students Pitch Their Writing Plans and Elicit Feedback from Their Peers

Intentional pairing for academic conversations Expanding multilingual learners, especially if they have been on the developing or expanding level for quite some time, might shut down if they are paired with students who express frustration as they search for the right words or take an extra moment to grasp readings. That's why it's important to intentionally pair them with students who will be patient and understanding. Intentional pairing can also include student choice—when students work with peers they feel safe with, they lower their guard and feel more relaxed about contributing their ideas.

One focus area for pair work is a three-part approach to academic conversations based on Zwiers' (2019b) work:

1. Build conceptual understanding by identifying key ideas and making foundational claims. (What are we talking about?)

2. Clarify key terms and supporting details. (Are we really talking about what we intend to talk about? What important details are there?)

3. Fill in information gaps. (We don't know what we don't know, but where do we suspect there are some possible missing pieces of information? What do we want to know?)

Holly Sawyer, National Board Certified and ESL teacher, ensures her students have ample opportunities to make sense of complex learning through student-to-student interactions (see Figure 4–23).

Figure 4–23 Students Interacting with Each Other in a Relaxed Environment

Station rotation with adaptations   In these rotations, small groups of students move from station to station to explore one topic from multiple angles through interconnected tasks, multiple learning tools, and lots of shared conversations. The first adaptation I recommend is to build on the intentional pairing strategy and place students with some of their regular learning partners to travel through the stations. The second adaptation is to purposefully scaffold student engagement at each station, thus ensuring equitable participation in the topic exploration.

Let's get started with a basic rotation consisting of three stations:

Station 1: At this station, you use *instructional scaffolding* as you initiate or direct a discussion activity, modeling your thinking, using linguistic scaffolds, and employing productive wait time.

Let's consider a lesson about the civil rights movement. At the teacher-directed station, you will lead a guided exploration of the principles of nonviolence, what they mean, why the leaders of the movement chose this path, and so on.

Station 2: Here you implement *digital scaffolding* through a carefully structured task that invites student collaboration online and offline as students work together to complete a task using a digital tool (such as a Google document).

At this station, students will work in pairs to identify changes that the civil rights movement have brought about and locate historical and contemporary images using several approved websites that show what has changed. A Google template will guide students in their search as well as in their caption writing for the images.

Station 3: At this station, *interactive scaffolding* is used in a collaborative activity that requires students to discuss and cocreate something.

Students will work in groups of four, with a specific role assigned to each member, to create a civil rights movement time line indicating key events.

You can expand the number of stations and the types of scaffolding that could best enhance students' receptive and productive language skills.

Expanding reading skills

Expanding level MLs need what all learners benefit from. Two ideas for supporting MLs with expanding their reading skills are (1) close reading strategies that include text annotations and questions on three levels of complexity (word, sentence, and text) and (2) jigsaw reading tasks with adaptations.

Annotating and interrogating texts on three levels   When you plan close reading for MLs, consider a short but rich selection of about 200–250 words. Although close reading can (and ultimately *will*) be completed independently, choose teacher-led explorations for MLs at the expanding level initially. Look for culturally relevant and engaging texts: students will be reading the text multiple times, and they need to stay enthusiastic and interested in the material. During the first reading, have students read for general understanding and for personal reactions. During the second, have students annotate the text, a technique that you'll need to model and explicitly teach MLs.

During the subsequent readings, have students answer increasingly more complex questions that address word-, sentence-, and text-level understanding, as shown in Figure 4–24. The goal is to move students from concrete, foundational questions first, to ones that integrate text comprehension with language features and their own thinking, and then to abstract and complex questions for critical analysis.

Combining jigsaw reading with academic conversations   The classic jigsaw technique has been around for quite some time; with some adaptations, it can be highly effective for expanding MLs. Students typically start in heterogeneous *base groups* of three to five members. The jigsaw sequence allows teams to engage in conversations based on individual and shared reading as they work on a complex assignment. Each group does different but related work. For example, they might all be analyzing the same text but with different lenses, or they might be discussing

	Questions to Support Close Reading		
	Concrete, Foundational, and Factual Questions	**Questions That Integrate Language, Thinking, and Text**	**Abstract and Complex Questions for Critical Analysis**
Discourse Dimension	What is the title of this reading? Look at the headings and subheadings: What do you infer/predict about the reading based on those text features? Look at the illustration on page X. What details stand out in the illustrations?	What is the main purpose of this author? What evidence is there that shows _____? Why did the illustrator choose to offer details on _____? How are those details also depicted in the text?	What is the theme of this selection? What message is the author trying to give the readers? What is the central idea or underlying message of the text? How does this passage compare to another literary piece we have read? How can you justify your answers?
Sentence Dimension	Which sentence introduces the topic? Which sentence identifies _____? Which sentence describes _____?	Which phrase or sentence helps the reader understand what the author means by saying _____? Can you find examples of where the author _____?	The text begins with _____. Why do you think the author chose to begin the text this way? The text ends with _____. Why do you think the author chose to end the text this way?
Word Dimension	What is the first important word in this text/paragraph? What does the word _____ mean in this context?	What words does the author use to describe _____? What words does the author use to convince the reader about _____?	Why did the author choose the word _____ to describe _____? What words stand out as carrying the most important piece of information?

Figure 4–24

different texts about the same topic. The students in each base group become specialists. Then, students leave their home groups to form *expert groups* with members from other groups. Each student brings their expertise from their base group to a wider discussion of the text or topic, thus putting the pieces of the jigsaw together through shared learning. After discussing the material or completing the task collaboratively, students return to their base group and take turns teaching their original group members what they have learned.

A Sampling of Ideas for Content Area Jigsaw Reading	
Literature/ELA	Expert groups read different selections of a thematic text set created by the teacher or co-created with students.
	Expert groups analyze class, race, and gender in *To Kill a Mockingbird*.
Social Studies	Expert groups study different primary source documents associated with a historical event, such as the collapse of the Soviet Union.
	Expert groups analyze the causes of World War 1 (militarism, alliances, nationalism, imperialism, assassination).
Science	Expert groups explore the four systems on Earth (biosphere, hydrosphere, geosphere, and atmosphere).
Math	Expert groups work on different but interconnected problems.
Art	Expert groups study Picasso's early work across four periods: The Blue Period (1901–1904), the Rose Period (1905–1907), the African-influenced Period (1908–1909), and Cubism (1909–1919).
Health	Expert groups read about five factors that may prevent drug and alcohol addiction.

Figure 4–25

You can effectively integrate multiliteracies, digital literacy, and visual literacy into the jigsaw tasks you are designing with MLs in mind as well.

Expanding writing support

Students at the expanding level of proficiency need opportunities to negotiate meaning in multiple different ways across different content areas. One challenge they need to face—and they are definitely up to it with your guidance—is to use writing *as a tool to learn* across the content areas.

Yuriko Gray, high school ENL teacher, offers lots of choices to her students for demonstrating their understanding of her units' essential questions. After reading *St. Lucy's Home for Girls Raised by Wolves*, by Karen Russell (2007), one of her students chose to create an illustrated book to respond to the following question: "How does adapting to a new culture impact the character over the course of the story?" See Figure 4–26 for some sample pages from her work.

Figure 4–26 Excerpts from a Ninth Grader's Creative Work

Freewriting   To increase fluency and comfort with writing, expanding level MLs need to write, and write a lot, without the fear of being corrected. Since mistakes are inevitable, some MLs at this level may become self-conscious and hesitate to deviate from examples or models you've offered. Freewriting encourages thinking with a pen, pencil, or keyboard, inviting students to generate a lot of ideas about an open-ended topic related to the class you are teaching in sentences that are as complete as possible. Students write without checking for spelling or grammar, without pausing and rereading what's on the paper or screen already, without the pressure of it being graded or even assessed. Sharing with others is optional to further encourage your students' willingness to express themselves. Let them regularly use a freewriting journal or a writing-to-learn journal so they can write with less academic anxiety.

Scaffolded note-taking   To help students learn how to participate independently in lessons that are based on observations and explorations, provide the necessary support by scaffolding their note-taking. Copying notes from the board is not considered writing for the sake of literacy development. Instead, support students in capturing their ideas; extracting main ideas and key details from what they see, hear, or read; and creating a shorthand for learning complex material.

Reading the genre to write in the genre   According to a well-established definition, genres are "categories or kinds of writing, with distinctive features or rhetorical elements that speak to their purpose" (Fearn and Farnan 2001, 227). Secondary MLs are exposed to a range of literacy tasks in their roles as readers and writers. Explicit knowledge of and experience with the major genre types help make academic language more visible and accessible. Genre knowledge enhances MLs' capacity with (1) understanding the purpose of the text; (2) recognizing the recurrent linguistic features of each genre; (3) being able to deconstruct and reconstruct texts across genres; and (4) developing original text in the target genre, first collaboratively with teachers and peers, then independently.

For the purposes of supporting MLs with their expanding literacy domain, I am building on work by Nell Duke et al. (2011), which organizes the reading and writing genres for a focused study into five major categories. (Similar genre families for key language use were also recently established by WIDA in 2020). Figure 4–27 provides a summary of these five major categories aligned to specific genre types, the purposes of the genres, select examples from secondary classrooms that integrate reading and writing, and suggestions on responding to expanding MLs' writing needs.

To support expanding level MLs in their writing across grade-appropriate genres, not only integrate appropriate print-based or multimodal texts as mentor texts but also consider taking an inquiry-based approach. When students are actively engaged in developing new understandings about each genre or text type, they develop deeper

Genre Groups				
Genre Groups	**Genre Types**	**Purpose**	**Examples from Secondary Classrooms**	**Meeting Expanding MLs' Writing Needs**
Narrative Genres	• Fictional narratives • Personal narratives • Memoirs • Biographies • Autobiographies • Family narratives • Community narratives	To share and to make meaning of experiences	Students read personal accounts of historical characters and write about real or imaginary events.	Choose texts in which MLs can see their lived experiences, and give them writing opportunities in which they can tell their personal stories, familial stories, and shared cultural stories.
Procedural Genres	• How-to texts • Protocols • Manuals • Directions for activities	To learn how to do something, to explain how something works, or to teach others how to do something	Students read science lab protocols and produce similar texts.	Invite students to construct "how-to" texts representative of their own expertise and funds of knowledge.
Informational Genres	• Reports • Research projects • Informational booklets • Informational websites	To develop and to communicate knowledge of a topic or expertise in a particular discipline area	Students read informational texts and online sources and write a research report or create a website about the topics they research.	Explicitly teach research skills. Offer mentor texts. Invite multimodal products.
Persuasive Genres	• Persuasive essays • Magazine articles • Formal letters and persuasive speeches • Advocacy projects • Pamphlets and posters	To articulate a claim and support it with evidence To affect change	Students read book or movie reviews and write their own. Students take a stand on a topic of choice and write an argument that includes a call to action.	Build on student in-school and out-of-school expertise. Teach word choices as well as sentence and paragraph structures for clarity of argument writing.
Dramatic Genres	• Plays • Scripts • Skits • Poetry	To explore meaning or to make sense of the world through creative and dramatic writing	Students read plays and scripts as well as write and perform short scripts or poetry (see Figure 4.28).	Invite students to express themselves via poetry and drama. Create opportunities to write creatively.

Figure 4–27 Adapted from Dodge and Honigsfeld (2014), Duke et al. (2011), and Honigsfeld and Dove (2022).

understanding, read with more comprehension and anticipation of what the genre is expected to represent, and write more effectively within each genre. Following is a spoken-word poem that eleventh grader Jimmy Ramirez Mejia created in an integrated ELA class co-taught by Loretta Schuellein-McGovern (ELA teacher) and Ashley Wong (ENL teacher). After a genre study, the teachers invited students to write and perform their own poems about a matter of great importance to them. Figure 4–28 shows the scaffolds Ashley provided for the poetry performance.

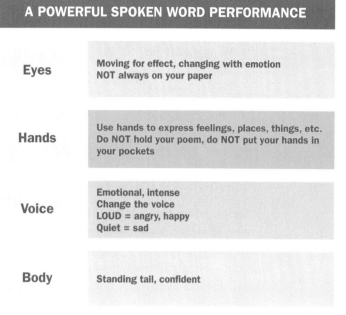

A POWERFUL SPOKEN WORD PERFORMANCE

Eyes	Moving for effect, changing with emotion NOT always on your paper
Hands	Use hands to express feelings, places, things, etc. Do NOT hold your poem, do NOT put your hands in your pockets
Voice	Emotional, intense Change the voice LOUD = angry, happy Quiet = sad
Body	Standing tall, confident

Figure 4–28   Guidance for the Spoken-Word Poetry Performance

ARE WE THE PROBLEM?

I've seen and heard how people in America think about Hispanics
They said we steal jobs
The jobs that they don't want
They said we ruined America
America has been ruined
It's a garbage dump piled high with injustice and prejudice
Make America great again they said
Are you sure we are the problem?
Racism in America
Racism in America
They hate us for no reason
They said we don't contribute
They said we don't help
But is that true?
I try to understand
But look at the jobs where Hispanics make up the majority
We farm for America
We take care of your forest

We build your houses
Maintain your gardens
Prepare your food
We give a lot too
I don't understand America
We give so much
We get tired from all the labor
My American Dream?
More like an American Nightmare.

Technology Integration

A variety of digital tools allow students to create digital content and practice, internalize, share, or demonstrate new learning. Students can work alone or with peers to research and create presentations with some commonly used tools such as PowerPoint, Google Slides, Canva, and Prezi, or you can help students venture into more versatile tools, such as creating an ebook or a ThingLink presentation, both of which incorporate audio, video, a range of different visuals, and texts. See Figure 4–29 for a summary of key digital tools that students can learn to use independently to study, complete research projects, or create presentations.

Digital Tools and Ways Students Can Use Them		
Digital Tool Type	**Examples**	**What Can Students Do?**
Productivity tools	Evernote, Notability	Take notes and organize ideas using new technology
Social learning platforms	Edmodo, Google Classroom, Edublogs, ePals, Twine	Write and produce digital content for authentic audience
Multimedia presentations	ThingLink, Prezi	Use multiple modalities to engage audience
Language and literacy building tools	Book Creator, EDpuzzle, Nearpod, Explain Everything, ShowMe, Imagine Learning Classroom, Discovery Education	Listen, read, view, and process through multiple modalities at their own rate of acquisition
Information-sharing tools	QR codes	Participate in or create scavenger hunts; share online resources

Figure 4–29

Digital Tools and Ways Students Can Use Them		
Digital Tool Type	Examples	What Can Students Do?
Simulation tools	Banzai! PhET	Learn about financial literacy, math and science through interactive simulations
Formative and self-assessment tools	Quizlet, Socrative, Kahoot!, Knowmia	Show their understanding and participate in new learning through gamelike activities

Figure 4–29 *Continued*

Notice When Expanding Level Students Are Ready to Move On

Although most schools determine levels of language proficiency and student placement based on annual standardized assessments such as ACCESS by WIDA, ELPA21, and NYSESLAT, formative assessments and progress monitoring play an important role in your day-to-day work with MLs. To track the progress expanding level students make, take a multidimensional approach. Your data collection should include teacher observations of oral language skills and student work samples to document how their writing skills have developed and reading conferences where you can check on their comprehension and also monitor how their reading skills are growing and to what extent they are able to apply reading strategies.

You will start noticing that expanding level students are bridging over to the next language proficiency level, which is referred to as bridging (no pun intended), when they can observe higher levels of fluency and accuracy in reading and speaking and more extended responses to questions posed orally or in writing.

Thinking back to the two students introduced at the beginning of the chapter, I expect that Janaína will learn to slow down her reading to deepen her understanding of not only the essential message of the text but important supporting details and some subtle nuances as well. She will continue to successfully access digital media while also expanding her skills to engage in more sustained discussions with peers and adults using varied, increasingly grammatically complex and longer sentences. Her writing will expand in length and complexity as she will be able to produce more detailed written responses to academic tasks.

parallel texts or text sets successfully while they continue to ᴧovels and digital recordings (both audio and video). With support and ᴧgement, they will participate in whole-class or other large-group discussions ᴧn more confidence. Their written work may continue to include some errors in word choice, grammatical structures, or organization but without any significant interference with conveying the intended meaning.

Chapter Five

Supporting

BRIDGING

Level Multilingual Learners

Meet *Bridging* Level Secondary Multilingual Learners

Let's meet Ruhi and Delun, two students who are at their bridging level of second language development. While their cultural, linguistic, and academic backgrounds and school experiences are are very different, they are both at the bridging level which means they have developed strong competencies when reading, engaging in personal and academic exchanges, and communicating both in writing and in speaking in English. The goal of this chapter is to offer some insights into further supporting students who have reached high levels of fluency and academic language competence, whether they have been declassified or not.

> No matter how full the river, it still wants to grow.
>
> —AFRICAN PROVERB

Ruhi

... seventh grade and has just ...ed the bridging level of language proficiency. She is originally from India, having arrived in the United States when she was in third grade. Her grandmother, who also came to the United States, is Ruhi's and her siblings' primary caretaker and speaks several languages and dialects. Nani ("grandmother" in Urdu) shows up to every school event and is very happy to support her grandchildren's education. Ruhi's mother is battling a chronic illness and her father travels a lot as a businessman; they are rarely seen at school, but they both try to attend parent-teacher meetings, scheduled twice a year, and are very pleased with their three children's academic success in school.

Ruhi has developed everyday conversational skills in English with ease and has demonstrated rapidly developing academic language proficiency ever since she first arrived in the United States. In New Delhi, she attended an English-medium school and she came with sound foundational literacy skills. By the time she completed her second year in a U.S. school, she was approaching fourth-grade level reading proficiency. Halfway through fifth grade, many of her teachers reduced the amount of modification for Ruhi and noted that some slightly adapted scaffolds would do the trick. To Ruhi's delight, her teachers recognized her potential and talent and placed her in small groups that offered challenges and enrichment opportunities in math, reading, and writing. She especially enjoyed the makerspace projects. In sixth grade, when she moved to the neighborhood middle school, she even ventured into running for student council (she was a close runner-up and is planning to run again next year).

As a seventh-grade student, Ruhi rarely leaves her classes for English language development support. She knows that her ELD teacher, Mrs. Suárez, regularly consults with several of her teachers and has biweekly conferences with Ruhi to check in on her assignments and troubleshoot when necessary. Ruhi is always excited to share what she is up to in her classes and is especially proud of reading the same chapter books her classmates are assigned. From time to time, she asks for help when she feels a bit lost regarding the context or the background knowledge needed for some readings. She is still working on making her writing more fully developed conceptually, richer in detail, and more cohesive with conjunctions and other text markers.

→ STOP AND REFLECT ←

What strategies could Ruhi's teachers use to help her with producing more complex written texts? How can they use her strengths to help her further improve in all areas of literacy?

Delun (Dé-Lún 德伦)

Delun is a high school senior originally from Shandong, a northeastern province in China. About two years before the 2020 COVID pandemic broke out, Delun's father was selected for an H1-B visa to work for a major technology company, which sponsored the whole family to relocate to California. Having only one child, Delun's parents were excited to move to the United States—to have great opportunities not only for themselves in the tech industry but for their son, too!

Soon after he started school in the United States, Delun began receiving praise for his hard work, brilliant mathematical mind, and quiet demeanor. Delun's parents saw this "model minority" myth in their workplaces, as well. They kept reminding their son to study hard, avoid any trouble or confrontation, and be an obedient young man. Delun took care of household responsibilities while his parents worked long hours. He gave up teaching people how to properly pronounce his name; not even sharing recordings of the correct pronunciation (via Voxifier) helped. In the end he simply accepted being called Dylan. In Chinese, his name roughly translates to "one who is fair (or just) to everyone," and it means a lot to him. But his mother reassured him, "Close enough, right? No need to get upset!"

But keeping his head down and not asking for help at school was counterproductive. His teachers and fellow students always assumed he was really good at math, but he was much more interested in the arts. His parents and other members of his extended family wanted him to go to an Ivy League school and become a bioengineer or to pursue a career in a STEM field. But once he was introduced to STEAM (science, technology, engineering, arts, math), he discovered digital arts to be his calling.

When COVID broke out, Delun worried about his safety, as some members of society and the media blamed China and Chinese Americans (or even *all* Asian Americans) for the pandemic. He was in his first year of high school when schools shut down, which significantly slowed down his progress with his expressive skills in English. Using Canvas, the learning management system his school introduced for remote learning, was an easy transition for Delun: he did all his reading and writing assignments on time and enjoyed the extra time he had to pursue his interest in digital design and art. He taught himself several free or low-cost programs, including Krita and MediBang Paint. He did not mind the independent research projects assigned in several of his classes, but he did not have much opportunity to talk to anyone in English. Now that school has been fully back in session for some time and he has been preparing his college applications, Delun is ready to challenge himself and focus on using English more.

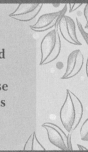

> → STOP AND REFLECT ←
>
> In what ways can Delun's teachers support him to use English more and more . . . and with more confidence and independence? How can they use his many areas of strength to address the challenges he might continue to face?

Look Beyond the Label

Language proficiency levels are never static. Your students may reach bridging level in some domains such as oral language skills as they are able to maintain conversations with fluency or read with confidence and deep understanding. Just because MLs at this level are advanced in their language acquisition, it does not mean these students no longer need support with language and literacy. At the same time, they may continue to experience challenges in one or more other domains; for example, they might have difficulties with organizing ideas when writing in an expository genre, presenting their report in front of a class, or reading complex texts across the disciplines.

Secondary ESOL teacher Tracy Jackson invites his students to engage in freewrites and to write imaginatively in preparation for academic writing tasks. Figure 5–1 shows a bridging level student's response to a prompt Tracy provided when the class was studying Maya Angelou's *I Know Why the Caged Bird Sings* (2015).

Achieving bridging level does not mean that students now read, write, and speak with full proficiency—because *no one* does! Figure 5–2 shows that the bridging level

Freewriting Helps Prepare Students for Academic Tasks

Teacher Prompt

Close your eyes; imagine that you are a bird living in a cage. What do you see? What do you hear? What do you smell and taste? How do you feel? Write for five minutes.

Student Response

I see a dark clouded sky, and the mahogany brown dead tree that has brittle bark and it started cracking. I can hear the tree branch breaking off the tree and the birds flying over me slowly if they are trying to mock me. I can smell the cold air the smell of the wet leaf's and the smell of the plants dying and rotting, it reminds me of fall. Alone stuck in a cage with my feet tied up. The feeling of nobody caring for me being alone in this darkness having all my emotion bottled up and all I can do is sing about freedom, the life I want. My feet are all cut up from the old ropes that's tied around my feet and to the cage. All I do is just dream about being free in the world and flying.

Figure 5–1

Other Labels for Bridging Level		
TESOL	**Hill and Miller (2014)**	**WIDA**
Bridging	Advanced fluency	Bridging

ELPA (2016)	**New York**	**California**	**Texas**
Proficient	Commanding	Bridging	Advanced high

Figure 5–2

of language proficiency has other labels, depending on the theoretical framework you refer to, the state or country you live in, or the language development standards you use.

The name suggests that the students are reaching an advanced level of proficiency that is often comparable to that of their English-proficient peers. Keep in mind that, as lifelong learners, they will not simply be done with English acquisition once they test proficient and may no longer receive specialized instruction or services in English language development. Instead, they will continue to thrive when they receive the right type of support and ample opportunities to further expand their language use.

Similar to Figure 4–2 in the previous chapter, the chart in Figure 5–2 also seems to suggest a close alignment. Most frameworks recognize that students at this level are at an advanced level of language development, metaphorically conjuring up the image of a bridge that connects these students to full competency with the language.

Consider What the Research Says

Among many other contemporary researchers, Valdés, Poza, and Brooks (2017) take a sociocultural approach to second language acquisition and describe the process as one that leads to *multicompetence* or *plurilingualism*, instead of someone becoming error free or speaking a language in the same ways that its monolingual speakers do.

Figure 5–3 All Students Need Continued Support

Recognizing that learners develop linguistic repertoires in multiple languages, Valdés and her colleagues challenge more traditional views that would describe the process of second language acquisition as a linear progression of merely acquiring a grammatical system and communicative competence in a new language. They also warn against articulating the goal of second language acquisition as becoming a *balanced bilingual*. They argue that a sociocultural perspective has the "potential of informing and enriching the design of classroom environments in which students would be able to experience multiple ways of using both their home language and English for a variety of academic purposes in both their written and oral forms" (70). Based on this philosophy, students at the bridging level will also be expected to use their rich repertoire of skills in multiple languages. However, they still need and appreciate continued academic, linguistic, and social-emotional support. Figure 5–3 shows a supportive poster that secondary EAL educator Alycia Owen created to encourage her students.

In addition, students at the bridging level are well characterized by what Hattie and Yates (2014) refer to as engaging in a deliberate learning process, which is slow in pace and does not often occur without sufficient time, focus, support, monitoring, and practice: "Impressions of quick learning are deceptive for many reasons. Unless the material is strongly meaningful, relevant and timely, it is subject to rapid and substantial forgetting" (113). More recently, Manuel Buenrostro and Julie Maxwell-Jolly (2021) have reported the critical need for teaching language and literacy across the core content areas and offering MLs consistent, carefully coordinated scaffolds so they can fully understand and use complex academic language. In sum, multilingual learners at the bridging level will benefit from multiple meaningful language and literacy experiences that challenge them; sustained opportunities to interact with the new academic material in English; and just-in-time peer and teacher support. See Figure 5–4 for the description of a collaborative project designed by Monica Starkweather, a secondary ESL teacher, and one of her colleagues. The description serves as a scaffold and reveals the teachers' high expectations for their students.

PROTEST: AN AMERICAN TRADITION

Objective: Students are required to research an American protest that occurred before this century and evaluate the protest using the guidelines discussed in class.

Requirements: Students must choose a protest from the list at the end of this document or propose one for <u>approval by the teacher</u>. Students must then complete the following:

1. Research your protest and <u>Complete the Protest Evaluation Worksheet.</u>

2. Read and Summarize "<u>2020 is not 1968: To Understand Today's Protests, You Must Look Further Back</u>" from National Geographic and write a one-paragraph summary of the article.

3. Compare your chosen protest with a protest or social movement that has occurred in <u>this</u> century. Examples include:

   - The March for Our Lives—March 24, 2018
   - Protests against police brutality in Ferguson, Minneapolis, Chicago, Portland, etc
   - Occupy Wall Street—Sept 17, 2011
   - Black Lives Matter Movement
   - Dakota Access Pipeline Protests—April 2016–Feb. 2017

4. Create a slide presentation

Protest Choices:

Newark Protest—1967

Trail of Broken Treaties Caravan—1972

Haymarket Affair—1886

The Delano Grape Strike—1965

Zoot Suit Riots—1943

Watts Riot—1965

The March on Washington for Jobs and Freedom—March 3, 1963

Stonewall Riots—June 28–July 3, 1969

Occupation of Alcatraz—Nov. 20, 1969–June 11, 1971

Greensboro Sit-ins—began in 1960

Million Man March—October 16, 1995

Protests at 1968 Democratic National Convention in Chicago

March for Equal Rights Amendment—July 9, 1978

Bonus Army—1932

Montgomery Bus Boycott—Dec. 1955–Dec. 1956

Figure 5–4   MLs Are Challenged to Engage with Complex Content

Understand Bridging Level Secondary Multilingual Learners

MLs who have reached the bridging level of language proficiency continue to represent a range of language and literacy skills across the four domains. Language acquisition is still fluid, individual, and ever changing, so continue to expect your MLs to demonstrate different levels of skills in listening, speaking, reading, and writing. In this chapter, we will continue the previously established assets-based exploration of what MLs can do and how their teachers can further support their growth. We must remember that language acquisition is a dynamic process that does not end when a learner achieves the highest level of language proficiency. As before, we cannot allow a label to define a student and must look at each ML as an individual learner.

A shared unique characteristic of bridging level students is their demonstrated success of acquiring advanced skills across all four domains: they can read and comprehend complex texts; they can express themselves orally and in writing across topics, both familiar and unfamiliar to them; and they maintain both personal and academic dialogues with increasing confidence. They can also take on leadership roles and support MLs at lower levels of proficiency as their role models and bilingual peer bridges. See Figure 5–5 for a page from the writing portfolio of Hexi Wong, a recent high school graduate, in which she shares her draft college application essay and her reflection on being a language learner.

When it comes to *listening*, you can expect evidence of high levels of English comprehension. Bridging level students are likely to be able to do the following:

→ understand main ideas, supporting details, speaker's purpose, and other more nuanced aspects of oral language

→ make most inferences based on what is presented orally

→ understand multistep directions

→ understand and respond to both everyday and academic conversations of increasing length and complexity

→ process digital recordings (both audio and video) with confidence

→ comprehend increasingly demanding, contextualized, and decontextualized oral presentations

→ attempt to make sense of unfamiliar colloquial expressions, cultural references, and idioms or proverbs

College Essay

With the airplane motor humming in the background, I slept through one dream after another until I woke up hearing my mother's voice. "Do you want to start recording your life in America? It will be very different from our past." This was the plane that took me from my birth country China to the US four years ago. Back then, I didn't realize the impact studying abroad would have on my life. I turned on my laptop and began typing my first words under the dim cabin light.

I've always loved writing from as far back as I could remember, perhaps through the influence of my journalist parents. Writing allows me to dig into an idea and observe details that would otherwise be overlooked, driving me to notice negligible facts with curiosity. After I arrived in the US, writing became a forum for me to reflect on moments filled with emotions, bound by both excitement and anxiety: Asking questions with sweaty hands, participating in gym classes without Wenzhou's strenuous 800-meter tests, and training as part of the youth corp in a volunteer community ambulance. Every new experience became rich material to share with not only my family and friends but also readers across oceans. Using WeChat, an online publishing platform, I shared my experiences with those outside my American community.

But I hadn't touched my pen to write in a long time.

As soon as I started communicating with people in the new environment, I realized the language barrier between me and my classmates. The inability to communicate with others manifested a sense of fear that motivated me to prioritize learning English. Consequently, I gradually wrote less than before, seemingly forgetting my former self. When anyone asked about my immigration experience, the best I could come up with was, "My English has improved quickly." But that response left me unsatisfied; I was surprised I couldn't recall more details. That's when I decided to revisit old memories preserved by my published articles.

I clicked on the first one, "Fire Drill, Autumn Color, and Scientific Thinking," where a school fire drill prompted me to observe the trees spread over the hills behind the football field. The piece told a story of a track painted with multitudes of warm colors. I conveyed my excitement to the biology teacher, who in turn joked about the colors being products of "carotenoids in chlorophyll."

After reviewing my article, tears began flooding my vision. When I first started documenting my arrival in America, I would unknowingly observe every detail around me, willing to sit on the couch for five hours recording the difference from my old school—the characteristics of the locker room, school bus, and cafeteria hidden in plain sight. But as I became busier with my new existence, I not only let my passion for writing slip but also lost part of myself. Skimming through more articles, I confirmed my time in America was beyond just learning English. As an international student, I have experienced a variety of new happenings, from beautifully fierce snowstorms to presentations at my teachers' union meeting. I began to appreciate my pieces not simply as an anthology for my readers, but as a representation of my growth as an immigrant, student, and writer. Through my writing, I reflect on those initial vestiges of an unconfident foreigner suffocating in cultural and linguistic differences, to an inspired student ready to engage in new experiences.

I talked about my interest in writing my college essay. I described my experience as an immigrant, my love of writing, and the motivation I gained from going over my writing pieces. During the college application round, I edited the essay with more details about how I went through the language barrier and how writing prepared me for college.

Figure 5–5   Sample Writing Portfolio Page with Student Reflection

Regarding *speaking* skills, you will notice that MLs at the bridging level will

→ participate in formal and informal conversations with confidence and clarity

→ speak fluently about familiar and academic topics in small- and large-group settings

→ maintain extended dialogues with peers and teachers

→ communicate fluently and spontaneously with minimal hesitation, self-correction, or rephrasing

→ use a comprehensive repertoire of sentence structures and complex grammatical structures

→ make phonological, syntactic, or semantic errors that don't impede the overall meaning of the communication

→ confidently offer prepared academic presentations

→ integrate a rich variety of grade- and age-appropriate words, including technical or colloquial expressions, yet may encounter challenges with figurative language such as metaphors, idioms, and proverbs as well as less commonly known idiomatic expressions

When it comes to *reading,* your bridging level students will demonstrate more complex skills as they begin to

→ read and understand texts on familiar as well as novel topics with appropriate speed and fluency

→ read for enjoyment and academic purposes with increased fluency

→ comprehend all main ideas and supporting details in increasingly complex academic texts

→ develop new learning by reading texts on unfamiliar topics

→ figure out meanings of new words and complex sentences using context clues and prior knowledge or other linguistic resources, although they will likely continue to find idiomatic expressions and words with multiple meanings challenging

→ make sense of complex texts using various comprehension strategies, occasionally requiring scaffolds and supports

With *writing*, bridging level students will be able to do the following:

→ effectively communicate ideas related to familiar and academic topics

→ write for personal and academic purposes with increasing fluency and length

→ demonstrate control over increasingly more complex grammatical structures, but may make errors in syntax and word choice

→ take notes based on information they read or listen to with increasing accuracy and detail

→ write in all major grade-appropriate academic genres (narrative, expository, persuasive) although they may continue to encounter challenges with discipline-specific vocabulary or complex sentence structures

→ organize ideas into logical, well-developed text with errors in word choice or grammar that do not interfere with meaning

→ produce written texts of various lengths and purposes with minimal errors that do not impede the overall meaning

See Figure 5–6 for an example of how Alycia Owen, secondary EAL educator, guides her students to explore shades of meaning.

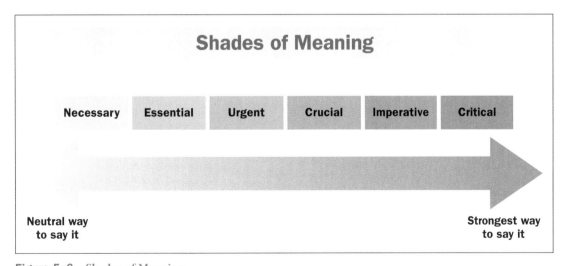

Figure 5–6 Shades of Meaning

In Eli Gomes' high school math class, students explore the intersection of math and other content areas. Figure 5–7 contains the introduction section of a bridging level student's essay on consonance and dissonance, connecting music theory and mathematics.

Overall, you will notice how bridging level students are becoming more independent and confident with their communicative language skills as well as with academic literacy skills. As a result, you will notice more active engagement in language and literacy tasks across a variety of grade- and age-appropriate academic settings.

Let's check back on Ruhi and Delun, whom you met at the beginning of the chapter. Although both are identified as bridging level students, their areas of strength and

Excerpt from a Student
Essay Titled "Modeling Consonance and Dissonance"

As a pianist and a singer, my life is surrounded by music. In the past thirteen years of music learning, I realized that math is an essential part of music, and I am always curious about the correlations between math and music. When I had my first piano lesson in kindergarten, I learned piano fingering and music score notations. Later, as I studied music theory, I discovered that almost everything in music is associated with math—key, tempo, time signature, rhythm, chords, intervals, and so forth. I wasn't sure about the relations between them back then with my limited knowledge in both areas, but I was indeed curious.

As I stepped into the IB [International Baccalaureate] Music course, I was introduced to the musical concepts of "consonance and dissonance". Consonance occurs when a combination of notes sounds harmonized. Vice versa, the unpleasant sound created by a combination of notes is called dissonance. As I studied music history, another musical concept evolved in the 19th century named "atonality" came into my vision. Atonality is a condition of music that sounds random and noisy to the audience. As I listened to atonal music, I was shocked by the dissonance, and I certainly didn't enjoy dissonance until I learned jazz music. Recently, I composed a jazz composition. I discovered that many jazz chords are constructed with both consonance and dissonance, and they sound surprisingly pleasant. Due to my passions for music and my curiosity about the concepts of consonance and dissonance, I decided to focus on this topic.

Since everyone has different musical tastes and auditory senses, it is challenging to objectively justify the concepts of consonance and dissonance. Nonetheless, I believe that even though music is subjective, math is highly logical and objective. Therefore, I decided to use math as a tool to help me find a logical explanation for why consonance and dissonance sound different.

Figure 5–7

their needs for further growth are quite different. Ruhi continues to enjoy reading and her favorite lessons are when students are asked to work in jigsaw groups. She takes great pride in being able to teach her classmates when—after some in-depth shared learning in expert groups—they all go back to their home groups to present what they have learned. Ruhi's teachers know that even students who are highly proficient MLs still need some linguistic scaffolds, such as outlines or discussion prompts, to continue to help them confidently share their new learning in English. Her writing is increasing in length, yet she is still working on gaining confidence with some text markers to make her writing more cohesive.

Delun, on the other hand, is working on becoming a more confident participant in small-group and large-group discussions. He appreciates every opportunity to express himself visually and present his thinking through art and design. He is proud to see his work displayed on bulletin boards in several content classes, and he knows his teachers have noted how talented he is.

Begin Here with Bridging Level Students

Although the broad-brush descriptions here will help you understand what your MLs can do, bridging level students need continued opportunities for academic language practice across all four domains. These students will be best supported through teaching techniques that appropriately challenge and affirm them linguistically and academically as well as socially and emotionally. They also need learning activities that encourage them to take further risks with the language and use their full linguistic repertoires in English and—whenever they wish to continue to use them—their home languages (rather than replace their first languages entirely).

Continue to enhance bridging MLs' comprehension of increasingly complex language and context and involve them in more complex, more precise, and more extended language production. Some practices designed to challenge bridging level MLs across all four language domains at the highest possible levels are (1) listening to and discussing podcasts and other digital recordings, (2) reading widely, deeply, strategically, and collaboratively, and (3) engaging in personalized learning opportunities focused on unique areas of need.

Listen to and Discuss Podcasts and Other Digital Recordings

Just as figuring out the lyrics to fast-paced music can be tricky, listening to rapid speech without visual support may present a challenge for all MLs, even those at the highest language proficiency levels. The photo in Figure 5–8, taken by one of Jason

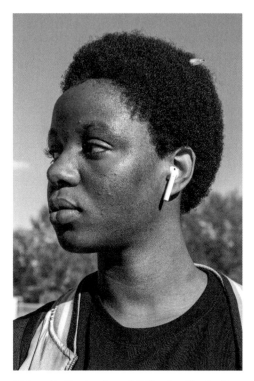

Figure 5–8 An Award-Winning Portrait, Taken by a Bridging Level Student

Raymond's multilingual learners at the Burlington Tech Center in Vermont, reminds us of how ubiquitous music, podcasts, and audio are in teens' lives. (The photo was also awarded third prize in the 2023 Vermont Congressional Art Competition.)

When an oral presentation or even a teacher read-aloud is lengthy or happens to be on an unfamiliar topic, bridging level MLs may disengage, lose focus, get stuck on some unfamiliar detail, or otherwise struggle with making all the necessary inferences or connections. Sometimes they might just need a little time out from English because learning a new language and reading, writing, listening, speaking, processing new information, and participating in fast-paced lessons in English can be exhausting. To build up stamina, begin with multimedia presentations that students at the bridging level may *view* and *listen to* at the same time. They can even use subtitles to further support their understanding. Some teacher-created examples are prerecorded Canva, Google, or PowerPoint slides or screencasts (for further suggestions, see the section on digital storytelling later in this chapter).

Podcasts or digitally recorded books present a unique opportunity for students to make sense of material that is delivered with limited or no visuals (Rubin, Estrada, and Honigsfeld 2022). Listening to stories that are intriguing, suspenseful, and personally relevant builds stamina for making meaning based on oral input. Rather than singling out MLs and separating them with a headset and a device, remember to make this a collaborative, socially engaging activity that requires students not only to listen but to discuss and deconstruct meaning as well as connect the listening to visually representing, writing, and further reading. You can also assign listening to podcasts or other digital audio recordings for homework, similar to flipped learning (discussed in Chapter 3). MLs may also benefit from guided note-taking tasks and discussions, such as the tool in Figure 5–9, which can also be adapted for in-class use.

Listening Directions and Guided Note-Taking Tool

Fill in specific information for each listening task:

As you listen to the episode about [topic], complete the following steps.

First Listening

1. Listen to the entire podcast without stopping or rewinding to get the gist of it.
2. When finished, jot down your answers to the following questions.
   a. What was the recording about?
   b. What else would you like to find out about [topic]?

Second Listening

3. Set the timer to [number of minutes] minutes. This is how much time you will have to listen to the podcast again and take notes. Listen to the podcast once more, and this time, feel free to stop the recording or rewind it as needed to be able to take notes in the following listening grid:

Question	My Answer
[Question 1]	
[Question 2]	

4. Use Flip to record your own ninety-second review of the podcast. Remember to include three main points in your review using our SEA acronym:
   a. **Summary:** What is the main message of the podcast?
   b. **Evaluation:** What was done well and what could be improved in this podcast?
   c. **Application:** How does the message of the podcast apply to you or to other listeners?

Figure 5–9

Encourage Reading Widely, Deeply, Strategically, and Collaboratively

When MLs at advanced proficiency levels have difficulty understanding complex texts, it may be caused by a lack of familiarity with the topic, people, events, or perspectives presented in the text. Some students continue to see a disconnect between their experiential pasts or current lived experiences and what they are asked to read and learn about. Tiffany M. Nyachae (2019) reminds us that many students (including MLs) have already developed critical consciousness and may frequently engage in critical discussions about topics of great importance outside of school; our job is to make sure that our schools and classrooms provides a safe space for such critical conversations.

Students at the bridging level will benefit from

- → reading across genres and topics (or reading widely),
- → using a critical and analytical lens (or reading deeply),
- → employing a prereading, during-reading and postreading protocol (or reading strategically), and
- → making reading social and dialogic (or reading collaboratively).

Working in neighboring districts, Neeley Minton (lead social studies coach) and Alicen Brown (coordinator of social studies and world languages) have been collaborating to offer more robust content instruction to multilingual learners. See Figure 5–10 for an example of how they ensure multiple types of scaffolding support are available to the students as they unpack a historical document, the Dunmore Proclamation of 1775, in sections. As the students explore what led up to the American Revolution, they engage in inquiry-based learning around the question *When should authority be questioned?*

Teach students to use a system to keep track of what they are reading and learning. The goal of this tool—whether you call it a reading log, a reading diary, a reading journal, or a response journal—is to give them a way to hold on to their ideas and to prepare them for critical discussions. You can design it to ensure students document what they understood in the text or what critical reflections and questions they had about it. You can either encourage students to write down some predetermined information (such as certain focal points) or, better yet, invite students to select their own ways of keeping track of their reading and documenting their thinking. Consider technology and multimodal ways of expressing new learning to motivate your students. See Figure 5–11 for technological tools that may augment or replace traditional paper-and-pencil reading logs or journals.

Content Vocabulary	**A PROCLAMATION**
	AS I have ever <u>entertained</u> Hopes that an Accommodation (agreement) might have taken Place
Academic Vocabulary	between Great Britain and this **Colony**, without being <u>compelled</u>, by my Duty, to this most disagreeable,
<u>Underline</u> things we don't know	but now absolutely necessary Step, rendered so by a Body of armed Men (men with guns), unlawfully assembled (forming a body of men with guns without
Definitions/synonyms	permission), firing on his Majesty's Tenders (shooting at the king's troops) . . .

Figure 5–10   Four Types of Scaffolds Support a Close Reading of the Dunmore Proclamation

Technological Tools That May Augment or Replace Traditional Written Response	
Technological Tool	**What the Tool Does**
Notability	Lets readers take notes directly in the app or scan in print pages (such as snapshots of pages from a book they read) and add text markups or annotations digitally.
LiveBinders	Keeps all reading logs together in one digital place.
Tellagami	Allows readers to create an avatar (character) and record responses to readings through digital voice recordings.
VoiceThread	Lets students record and share responses to readings through digital voice recordings.
Book Creator	Lets learners combine text, images, and video and audio responses to readings.
Green screen technology	Allows students to create professional-looking edited videos.

Figure 5–11

Students at the bridging level will benefit not only from reading widely (to further expand their background knowledge and to build new frames of reference) but from reading deeply as well (to develop expertise in unique topics of interest and to foster curiosity and motivation for more independent reading).

Analytical skill building is frequently incorporated in the secondary curriculum. There are several helpful scaffolds to guide students to deeper understanding and to ensure they take a critical stance regarding what they are reading. CER is one useful formula students can use to analyze nonfiction pieces and to use some of the readings as mentor texts for their own writing:

→ **Claim:** What are the claims, stances, positions, or opinions presented in the text?

→ **Evidence:** What types of data, facts, information, or detail are provided?

→ **Reasoning:** How effectively does the author explain the connection between the claim and the evidence?

Among others, Sharroky Hollie (2017), Gholdy Muhammad (2020, 2023), Mary Ehrenworth, Pablo Wolfe, and Marc Todd (2021), Don Vu (2021), and Kimberly Parker (2022) have emphasized the need for historically, culturally, and linguistically responsive and civically engaged literacy and learning experiences that support criticality. Gholdy Muhammad (2023) defines *criticality* as

a way to ask students to evaluate and dismantle systems of oppression (including, but not limited to, racism, sexism, classism, ageism, xenophobia, ableism, homophobia, and others). Criticality builds social-political consciousness, so students are not passive learners, but rather emphatic, critical thinkers, working to see, name, and root out discrimination and oppression in all forms. (75–76)

See Figure 5–12 for an example of how Andrea Dell'Olio, secondary ENL teacher, invites her students to read about, discuss, and analyze complex societal issues, practice criticality, and also develop advanced language skills by evaluating and responding to high level, thought-provoking questions.

When students read strategically, they employ a range of *before-*, *during-*, and *after*-reading strategies. These may include (1) previewing the reading to help situate the text, activate prior knowledge, pose questions, and make some predictions; (2) while reading, utilizing stop-and-process strategies that support getting the gist of the reading paragraph by paragraph and allow for fix-ups in meaning making as

Students Practice High-Level Questioning Through Criticality

Directions: Look at the following questions and write a check if the question is a high level, thought-provoking question. Then, write at least two possible responses to prove it is a high-level question.

Question:	High-Level Question?
1. *How is racism still affecting all of us today?*	
Two possible responses: 1. 2.	
2. *Is it acceptable for some schools to be segregated today?*	
Two possible responses: 1. 2.	
3. *How could educational experiences affect who we become later in life?*	
Two possible responses: 1. 2.	
4. *How can we stay true to our identities no matter who our audience is or where we are?*	
Two possible responses: 1. 2.	

Figure 5–12

the students look inside and outside the text for clues; and (3) reviewing the text to consolidate understanding, to summarize, and to engage in further reading, writing, or discussions about the text.

Reading collaboratively adds yet another opportunity to motivate teenagers to read, to share the literacy experience (and their opinions) with peers, and to engage in further communication about the text. Inquiry circles or literary clubs (sometimes referred to as literature circles) make MLs more socially connected to their peers as they participate in shared meaning making, explore multiple perspectives, question each other, and reflect on their own thinking. When they closely examine, dissect, or even interrogate the concepts and beliefs presented to them in print or by some other form of representation, they develop their autonomy as thinkers and learners. Here is a set of question starters for your students to use:

→ Why are . . .?

→ How did . . .?

→ What caused . . .?

→ What led to . . .?

→ What is meant by . . .?

→ What is the relationship between . . .?

→ Why must . . .?

→ What would happen if . . .?

→ What will the result be . . .?

→ Would the result have been different if . . .?

→ What will the future be like for . . .?

Reading for enjoyment and developing lifelong reading and writing habits are just as important as reading for academic purposes. Do you know what constitutes your students' literary lives? What captivates them? What is most meaningful to them? Are they drawn to current events, are they interested in science fiction, or do they look to the past and enjoy historical fiction? According to Pahl and Pool (2021), *hopeful literacies* move readers away from the present into a possible or imagined future so as to focus on what could be. Also remember, we live and teach in the age of multiliteracies: we are no longer confined to print (Kim and Belcher 2020), so let's encourage students to read for enjoyment by making available a wide range of high-interest print-based and online reading materials such as digital subscriptions, poetry, song lyrics, young adult novels, comic books, sports and other teen magazines, and so on. Many of Jason Raymond's multilingual learners are passionate about digital art and photography. Jason, the digital media lab teacher at the Burlington Tech Center, invites his multilingual students to create authentic digital art connected to their realities or representing their identities. He is committed to creating a learning space that is aligned to students' strengths and challenging students to work on projects of substance. Figure 5–13 is a photo one of his students took. Titled *Selfie Mirror*, the photo was selected for the Vermont Congressional Art Award in 2021.

Figure 5–13 *Selfie Mirror*, Taken by Patient Mwibeleca

Focus Personalized Learning Opportunities on Students' Needs and Interests

Expect bridging level students to begin to thrive using increasingly complex language while continuing to be challenged by unfamiliar language patterns, unique language features, and conceptual complexity when they read grade level academic texts, listen to others, or try to express themselves orally and in writing. They might have become very good at guessing some word meanings, figuring out increasingly longer sentences, and getting the gist of texts (whether presented in a print format or orally). Yet they are very likely also to encounter words, sentences, and texts that are not fully comprehensible and thus remain confusing or disconnected for them. The rich and highly specialized vocabulary, the syntactic complexity, and the density of texts presented across a variety of topics and genres may present challenges to the most proficient MLs. In addition, we need to pay attention to these conceptual level characteristics:

→ developing language skills for a range of cognitive functions (such as describing, analyzing, evaluating, and synthesizing)

→ understanding and communicating about abstract concepts

→ offering adequate details in writing and speech

→ maintaining objectivity by separating the speaker from the subject and employing logical reasoning

Secondary ENL and world language teacher Justine Hernandez offers individualized opportunities for exploration in her class, where this year the seventeen UN Sustainable Development Goals served as springboards for design thinking projects. Her bridging level student wanted to explore ways to reduce paper consumption within the context of UN Goal 12: Responsible Consumption and Production. According to the first few steps of the design thinking protocol, students are expected to look, listen, and learn, generate a lot of questions, and start to understand and frame a problem they wish to address (Spencer and Juliani 2020). Figure 5–14 shows select areas of exploration, with Justine's student's own questions and the preliminary answers he generated based on his research.

Bridging Level Student's Digital Notes
Based on the Design Thinking Protocol

1. *How Wood Turns to Paper*

- How many pages of paper can we make per one tree? *10,000 sheets (I am surprised)*
- Where did people find the acids and minerals to make paper? *sulfite salts with an excess of sulfur dioxide*
- Where was the first paper made? *Paper originated from China and was created by Ts'ai Lun*
- Can paper be replaced? *People haven't thought of any change to paper*
- How many trees do we use for paper each year? *from 4 billion trees to 8 billion trees*

2. *How It's Made: Paper Recycling*

- Is there an easier way to turn old paper into new? *Yes there is*
- Why can't we always reuse paper as the video showed us? *Every time paper is recycled, its fibers break down a little.*
- Why can't we use technology instead of paper? *Using paper is one of the most effective ways to study and retain information*

3. *Our Forests: Time Lapse*

- What are the effects of deforestation? *Climate change, desertification, soil erosion, fewer crops, flooding, increased greenhouse gasses in the atmosphere, and a host of problems for Indigenous people.*
- How can deforestation affect animals or plants? *It causes habitat destruction, increased risk of predation, reduced food availability, and much more.*
- Are methods that are used to cut trees eco-friendly and safe? *Regeneration methods include clearcutting, shelterwood, and seed tree cuts*

Figure 5–14

Justine shared that this student-led exploration began with the simple idea of *reduce, reuse, recycle.* Ultimately, the product was much more comprehensive, including physical examples of realistic and easily obtainable sustainable or biodegradable alternatives to items that the community regularly used. This project raised awareness within the school community about the fact that they were all able to make more eco-conscious decisions that would positively impact our planet (see Figure 5–15 for an exhibit in the main lobby of the school).

Figure 5–15   A Table Display Showing Student-Designed Project Prototypes with Their Respective Sustainability Facts

Another way to ensure that students seek deeper understanding and receive continued, personalized support from you is to identify the unique areas of strength and need they have and coconstruct pathways to where the students want to be and see themselves being. Bridging level students have practiced goal setting and self-monitoring, and most likely, they have been using their metacognitive and metalinguistic skills (check back to Chapter 4 for a recap). When remote learning was over, Johanna Paraiso (2022) used Google Hangouts not just for students to share their senior research with each other and with students in other schools but also for holding small-group conferences after school once a week to check in on their comprehension of a complex topic or give feedback on their work in a safe, more private session.

Focus on Multidimensional Strategies

Following is a selection of multidimensional instructional practices and strategies for supporting bridging level students, organized into four main strands: (1) social-emotional support; (2) experiential learning support; (3) support across multiple modes of communication (including supporting visual literacy, building oracy, and building literacy); and (4) technology integration. Keep in mind that you can use many of these strategies with all levels of language proficiency, so as you read through the book, try to avoid limiting your strategy use to the designated language proficiency level where the strategy is first introduced.

Social–Emotional Support for Adolescent MLs

In an artistic essay rich with student work and dialogues, Fiona Blaikie (2020) aims to uncover that in-between, liminal space where adolescents need "to be, become, and belong" in the world (344). As your MLs are bridging to full capacity with the English language, they may find themselves in that in-between space; they may continue to question their belonging and not-belonging; their becoming fully recognized for their linguistic competence while at the same time possibly experiencing language loss or less opportunity to continue to develop academic language skills in their primary language. As teenagers, they are also grappling with who they are, so continue to support them not just linguistically and academically but socially and emotionally as well. As your students reach higher levels of proficiency in English, they might also reach a new level of understanding of *who to be* and *how to be* in this new language and world. A possible support system during this process is to offer mentoring to multilingual students, especially in areas of in- and out-of-school learning and enrichment opportunities, college and career choices, scholarships, post–secondary school planning, and so on. When your MLs grow up in homes where parents are in survival mode, or if they are not fully familiar with school norms and expectations in the United States, someone has to show them the ropes.

Here are some generic and more specific tips on what to keep in mind as you design a mentoring program or initiate mentoring relationships on a smaller scale:

→ **Mentoring should begin well before MLs hit the bridging level.** Remember that many strategies in this book cut across proficiency levels, and mentoring may benefit MLs differently when they first arrive or when they are ready to move on to a new level—any level!

→ **Family customs and cultural norms (including relying on extended family members or defining gender roles differently)** may present as barriers or may lead to misunderstandings. The mentoring initiatives must be carefully planned, introduced, and launched with family and student buy-in.

→ **Peer mentoring can be a powerful alternative to educators offering the mentoring support.** Consider both cross-age and cross-cultural as well as same-age, near-age, and monocultural pairings, especially in cultural contexts where adults outside the family rarely step into a mentoring role.

→ **Mentors should listen and smile more.** Always start by understanding the strength, resilience, and courage it took immigrant families to leave their homes and start a new life in the United States.

→ **Mentors are learners, too.** Take every opportunity to understand your mentees' cultural backgrounds, historical perspectives, and lived experiences.

→ **Your bridging level students themselves can become mentors.** They are likely to grow into a perfect position to serve as powerful cultural brokers and language mediators for younger students or newcomers in the same school context.

Starting level students in Terrence Walters' secondary social studies class regularly work with more proficient learners. In Figure 5–16, some of his students are discussing their notes on Andrew Jackson's presidency to determine which elements are of significance. Terrence has found that it helps all his students to process what they are learning when they can take an active part in the lesson by talking, sharing, and thinking together.

Experiential Learning Support

Digital storytelling and multimedia projects inspired by maker education may lead to new and exciting opportunities for student self-expression. These technology-enhanced learning approaches allow students at all proficiency levels to express themselves in multimodal and multilingual ways. Digital storytelling and multimedia projects tap into this reality.

Digital storytelling and podcasting

Since time immemorial, storytelling has been and continues to be a uniquely human endeavor. Nigerian

Figure 5–16 Bridging Level Students Benefit from Supporting Their Peers

storyteller Chimamanda Ngozi Adichie explains in her 2009 TED talk "The Danger of a Single Story":

Stories matter. Many stories matter. Stories have been used to dispossess and to malign, but stories can also be used to empower and to humanize. Stories can break the dignity of a people, but stories can also repair that broken dignity.

Traditional storytelling and narrative writing are powerful ways to have MLs communicate and tell their stories, or if they choose to amplify other people's voices, they can tell even more unheard stories for all to learn from. When students engage in digital creation, it adds a new dimension to these literacy practices. As a result, students can also exercise digital citizenship as well as develop a range of authentic, twenty-first-century literacy skills that require technology integration. Brett Pierce (2022) identifies five key components of impactful digital storytelling that help students practice and produce in this genre. I am inviting you to also consider some key language and literacy development scaffolds and tools that MLs can use to uniquely enhance their experiences through these five elements:

1. **The hook:** Ask a lot of questions, brainstorm and bounce ideas off others, and select the one question that generates a lot of interest and excitement.

2. **Visual moment:** Use sketchnotes or other visual representations for initial ideas; storyboard your narrative to be better prepared for telling your story and telling it visually.

3. **Sound moment:** Experiment with multiple language-based and non-language-based sound effects; don't shy away from using music, songs, and dramatic effects (including the impact of pauses or longer periods of silence).

4. **Character:** Take your time to build your character and map out their journey. Create graphic organizers such as flow maps that show not only what they do but reveal all the decisions that the character(s) face in the digital story.

5. **The outtakes:** Save your drafts, celebrate your mistakes, and create a short combination of bloopers and other mishaps.

Multimodal, visually enhanced, or digital storytelling allows for adolescent MLs to talk about their lives, including their immigrant experiences. Check out the following online resources for possible models for your students as well as possible submission places for their stories:

→ The Immigrant Story

→ The Immigrant Learning Center

→ Green Card Voices

→ Immigrant Stories, hosted by the University of Minnesota

→ Migrant Child Storytelling

→ Suitcase Stories, hosted by the International Institute of New England

→ Made into America: Immigrant Stories Archive

→ My Immigration Story

In addition to personal narratives, students may use digital tools, especially podcasting, for expository and persuasive genres as well. Alycia Owen, experienced secondary EAL educator, says that "digital storytelling is perfect for capturing a lab experiment, personal reflections, learning portfolios, describing a process, questioning a concept, comparing/contrasting, revealing an argument, writing a biography, and so on" (personal communication, June 20, 2023). Storytelling and digital reporting come alive when oral presentations are supplemented with carefully designed slides rich with photographs, images, voice-over recordings, sounds, and animation. Secondary EAL specialist Lindsey Fairweather integrates digital literacy into her classes. After brainstorming collaboratively, each student creates a plan for the digital work they will create. Here's one example of an outline that guides students' projects about their own academic background, experiences, and goals.

→ Make a little video introducing myself, my experiences, and [school name]

→ IB learner profile

→ My goals

→ Last but not least: what I love about London

Support Across Multiple Modes of Communication

Secondary bridging level MLs continue to benefit from challenging yet affirming opportunities to participate in communicative practices that advance their language and literacy development. Once they reach this level, they are approaching proficiency and may present themselves the same as their English-speaking peers do. Yet keep in mind that the nuances of language and literacy development continue for a long time, so support that is contingent with students' unique needs will be most beneficial.

Supporting visual literacy

Visual support continues to be important for bridging level students; however, there are now new opportunities to enhance these students' visual literacy skills. While many adolescents are drawn to *dynamic* media (such as computer animation, videos, and digital recordings with sound effects), here I invite you to continue utilizing *static* media in a dynamic way through infographics.

Throughout the book I have suggested using visuals to build receptive or interpretive language skills as well as support students' expressive skills through visual modalities. By design, infographics are vibrant, complex visual tools that intentionally and carefully combine illustrations such as diagrams, photographs, charts, and graphs with limited amounts of text so readers can process and interpret numerical data trends alongside informational text. Infographics lend themselves to accessing and analyzing complex information presented in your classroom. Students can also create infographics as a way to report on their research or to issue a call to action about a topic. Stephen Noonoo (2023) also points out how infographics are ideal tools to build media literacy, critical thinking skills, and creativity. I agree with Jennifer Smith and Marla Robertson (2021), who suggest that it is essential for students to learn to interpret how graphics and text work in tandem to convey a message, to inform, or to persuade. See Figure 5–17 for an example of a digital sketchnote by Hexi Wang, a student in Dan Weinstein's high school creative writing course. Hexi used this highly visual format to capture her reading goals for her senior year.

Continuing to grow oracy: Socratic seminars

Socrates is well known for his use of questions to help his disciples think critically and arrive at their own answers. Through a contemporary version of Socratic circles or Socratic seminars, your students can learn to take ownership of the classroom discourse by contributing both questions and answers, thinking critically, and articulating their own thoughts and answers in response to what others have said. Practice in these skills is crucial for today's adolescents, who are bombarded with information through instant access to technology. As a formal, meaning-focused academic discussion based on a shared text, multimedia source, or work of art, a Socratic seminar is ideal for talking about content and language while at the same time supporting MLs' oral language development, including both active listening and speaking skills.

Figure 5–17 Reading Goals Captured as a Sketchnote

During Socratic seminars, students are typically divided into two groups, the inner and the outer circle, with each assuming different roles: the inside circle is the discussion group and members of the outside circle observe the discussion and take notes. However, a whole range of other configurations are possible, too, such as one whole-group circle, multiple smaller circles, and two sets of inside and outside circles taking place simultaneously (Spencer 2022).

The Socratic seminar helps MLs at the bridging level further develop their listening, verbal, and critical thinking skills. Many of your students will continue to benefit from anchor charts with academic language and sentence frames displayed in the room; if your MLs wish to refer to them during a discussion, make sure scaffolds are available. Participating and meaningfully contributing to classroom discourse offer students opportunities to assert themselves as leaders in the classroom and shift their position from one that requires assistance and support to one that clearly indicates potential. Keep in mind, though, that you do not have to wait until students reach the bridging level to help them claim their place in the classroom as students of potential, promise, and success!

While there are dozens of ways to run a seminar, the following step-by-step suggestions will help keep things simple at first:

1. Decide what text students will read.

2. Provide a graphic organizer for students to fill in as they begin to work in small groups to ask and answer text-dependent questions.

3. Cocreate some anchor charts with sample question starters for clarifying, adding on, and questioning. (You might also provide a copy of these question starters to each student for individual use.)

4. Decide how small groups will come together with the rest of the class to use the inner-outer circle format to interact with each other, to share and deepen their learning, and to evaluate each other. For example, they might

   - send one representative from their team to debate or discuss the issue in the middle of the class *or* come to the inner circle as a team

   - replace their representative in the inner circle with a different member of the group once the first representative has spoken twice

   - use talking chips to encourage participation: each student gets a certain number of tokens that they need to use up during the seminar, and each time they take a turn, they hand in a chip (This also prevents some students from dominating the conversation.)

Figure 5–18 shows how secondary ENL teacher Amanda Haleiko sets clear guidelines for students to participate in Socratic seminars.

Continuing to grow reading skills

Students at the bridging level of language proficiency have mastered all the foundational reading skills as well as comprehension skills that allow them to meet the typical requirements of grade level literacy tasks. However, there can be a significant difference when students read in a science class versus in social studies or math. Shanahan and Shanahan (2008) were among the first to define literacy instruction by distinguishing among three levels of literacy. In their framework, level one, or *basic literacy*, refers to understanding letter-sound correspondence, decoding, and accessing high-frequency words that are necessary for all reading tasks. Level two,

Socratic Seminar Discussion Protocol

- [ ] **Speaker 1** starts the discussion by referencing an image and using three words from the list to explain the connection made between the text and image.

- [ ] **Speaker 2** uses two words from the list to respond to speaker 1 and builds on their idea and then asks one question.

- [ ] **Speaker 3** answers the question using one word from the list and explains the connection between the discussed idea and an image.

- [ ] **Speaker 4** poses a question that relates to the image and answers the question using two words from the list.

- [ ] **Speaker 5** presents a counter argument to the answer presented using three words from the list.

Figure 5–18 Socratic Seminar Discussion Protocol

or *intermediate literacy*, designates skills that are common to many reading tasks, such as developing basic fluency when reading, understanding generic academic words and phrases, and applying general comprehension strategies to everyday and academic readings. Level three, or *disciplinary literacy*, specifies literacy skills that are essential to understanding and producing text that is unique to the various content areas: literature, history, science, mathematics, music, or any other subject matter.

To successfully navigate rigorous core content readings, MLs benefit from opportunities to engage in higher level literacy tasks that challenge them to integrate multiple literacy roles. Some key strategies for MLs to practice these literacy roles with a special focus on disciplinary literacy include text multiplication and the use of authentic reading material as well as an integrated, functional content and language analysis.

Text multiplication and the use of authentic materials   Text pairing has been well established for elementary classes. It supports the idea that students should explore a topic by reading at least two different selections related to each other: students read a fiction and a nonfiction piece on the same topic, thus developing a deeper appreciation for the text features of each type of text. To challenge and further expand the literacy skills of secondary students at the bridging level, develop a system for not just pairing but quadrupling or multiplying texts. In addition to your instructionally paired texts, locate several additional real-life reading selections and authentic literacy experiences. They can be websites, news articles and opinion pieces, blogs, contemporary literary fiction and poetry, political cartoons, advertisements, food labels, song lyrics, manuals, charts, and diagrams. Consider the following web-based resources that offer student-friendly, safe content for adolescent readers:

→ *YouthComm* (online magazine by Youth Communication)
→ Scholastic magazines for secondary students (including *The New York Times Upfront*, *Scholastic Action*, and *Science World*)
→ TED-Ed (TED's youth and education initiative)
→ ThinkTV (via PBS Learning Media)
→ AwesomeStories (a collection of thousands of original stories on a range of topics)
→ WatchKnowLearn (free pre-K–12 educational videos organized by theme)
→ The Florida Center for Instructional Technology's digital content for the classroom (a wide array of content spanning all grade levels)

Integrated, functional content and language analysis   Instead of taking a traditional approach to grammar instruction that focuses on parts of speech, subject-verb agreements, and sentence structures, proponents of a functional approach to language emphasize the need to explicitly teach the role language plays in content area texts in supporting students further in their literacy development. I have adapted and built upon Zhihui Fang's (2020) and Luciana de Oliveira's (2023) frameworks for an integrated, functional content and language analysis to advance bridging MLs' literacy skills so they can more deeply engage with disciplinary texts.

1. Context:
   - Content-based analysis: What background knowledge and experiences do students have about the topic? What additional contextual understandings do they need?
   - Language-based analysis: What linguistic resources and prior language experiences do students have? What previously acquired language skills can students build upon?

2. Target text:
   - Content-based analysis: What is the text telling us about the topic? What is happening? Who, what, when, where, why, and how . . .?

- Language-based analysis: What elements of language or special language features support the core message of the text, based on a paragraph-by-paragraph (or sentence-by-sentence) analysis?

3. Organization:
   - Content-based analysis: How is the text organized? How does the author present their ideas in a logical way?
   - Language-based analysis: What language features contribute to a logical organization of the text? What text markers create cohesion within each paragraph and within the entire text?

4. Perspective:
   - Content-based analysis: What is the author's primary purpose, perspective, and potential bias?
   - Language-based analysis: What word choices and other rhetorical devices does the author use to express their attitude toward the topic?

Alycia Owen, secondary EAL educator, noticed that her students were using the word *show* excessively (albeit accurately!). See Figure 5–19 for the tool she created to help them explore different wording options while also recognizing the subtle differences of the alternatives.

The author uses simile to **show** the similarities between two characters.

Our data **show** that more than three-fourths of our students participate in sports or clubs.

More customers are visiting the Spirit Shop. This may **show** that their advertisement in the newsletter was effective.

Try saying the sentences another way by replacing **show(s)** with:

- **demonstrate(s)**
- **illustrate(s)**
- **reveal(s)**
- **indicate(s)**

Figure 5–19   A Language-Based Analysis Helps Students with Word Choice

Continuing to grow writing skills

Similar to reading, the expectations for what types of writing secondary MLs typically engage in will vary based on the content area. Let's pause for a moment to reflect on the many writing tasks MLs encounter and how different these genres are: producing a lab report in science based on an experiment, developing a document-based analysis in social studies, writing an argumentative essay in ELA, and so on! Wondering what types of writing support you can plan for? Figure 5–20 shows how secondary EAL educator Tan Huynh scaffolds a task for students to analyze the validity and limitations of a source when researching complex contemporary topics. Notice the explanations in the left margin that justify each step. Keep in mind that at this level of proficiency, the scaffolds, supports, individualized feedback, and conferring will also vary greatly based on individual needs.

Offer specific feedback   For writing to improve, MLs need to share and receive feedback on their writing. The feedback should encourage them to reflect on their

ORIGIN: Is it a primary source or secondary source? Where did the source come from? Who created it? When was it created? What do you know about the author/creator? Is the creator an authoritative source?

Prompts (in parentheses) to guide students thinking.

The origin of this source is a (type of document) that was (written/presented on) (date of source & location if there is one) by (author). One aspect that makes the source valuable to historians is [select one; delete the rest] (the author, publisher, type of document, date of publication). An example from the source is [provide the example in our own words]. Historians would find this detail a value because [write 2 sentences max].

Embedded reminders within the paragraph frame [in brackets] to structure the output so that it's more accurate.

However, historians would find [select one; delete the rest] (the author, the publisher, the type of document, the date of publication) a limitation. An example from the source is [provide the example in our own words]. Historians would find this detail a limitation because [write 2 sentences max].

Figure 5–20   Scaffolding Students' Writing and Critical Thinking Skills

own writing and revise while paying attention to word choice, sentence structure, paragraph organization, and meaning (Anderson 2018). There are multiple ways to offer feedback on student writing:

→ Conduct regular writing conferences. Sit with students one-on-one and get to know them as writers. Try to articulate students' strengths and teach specific strategies that will help improve their writing.

→ Offer written feedback. Students sometimes want to take time to read and reflect on your feedback. Ask students if they would prefer comments directly in their notebook or paper or on sticky notes.

→ If students use digital writing tools, use marginal comments and track changes to offer students alternative ways of expressing the same thought.

→ Teach students to offer each other feedback. You can scaffold their partner work with some sentence stems posted on an anchor chart or printed on a piece of paper:

- When I read this part, I wanted to know more about _____.

- What more would you want your readers to know about _____?

- I noticed _____ and I wondered _____.

- Could you include more details on _____?

- Could you make connections to _____ here?

→ When I read this part, I had a question about _____.

Technology Integration

In late 2022 and early 2023, emerging technologies in support of language and literacy development were dominating English language development discourse. Professional blogs, social media feeds, newsletters, and even some research journals and magazines seemed to be filled with articles about the potentially harmful or potentially effective—but certainly inevitable—impact that artificial intelligence (AI) will have on teaching and learning. Virtual reality, augmented reality, and mobile learning tools are not new to language pedagogy: Google Translate, Duolingo, and

Babbel are just a few well-known tools that use AI. Now, GPTs (generative pretrained transformers)—especially ChatGPT and similar open-access tools—have taken our educational world by storm. In conversation with secondary educators, I have found that a consensus is growing: let's not ban their use; instead let's find creative ways to integrate them into the teaching and learning process and offer practical suggestions to further support MLs' learning.

One area in which ChatGPT and other AI tools hold the promise of helping is personalized feedback, which I was just discussing in the previous section. To illustrate this point, I pretended to be a student and asked ChatGPT to help generate prompts I could use to get feedback on written work or help improve my writing. This is how our exchange went:

My prompt: *How can I prompt you to improve my writing?*

ChatGPT's response: *To improve your writing, you can provide me with a piece of your writing and ask for specific feedback or suggestions. Here are a few ways to prompt me for assistance in enhancing your writing skills:*

1. **Request general tips:** *"Can you provide some tips to improve my writing?"*

2. **Ask for feedback on a specific piece:** *"Could you review this paragraph I wrote and offer suggestions for improvement?"*

3. **Seek advice on a particular aspect:** *"How can I enhance the flow and organization of my essay?"*

4. **Ask for assistance with grammar and vocabulary:** *"Can you help me identify any grammatical errors or suggest alternative words in this sentence?"*

5. **Inquire about writing techniques:** *"What are some effective ways to make my writing more engaging and captivating?"*

Feel free to use any of these prompts or tailor them to your specific needs. The more specific and detailed your request, the better I can assist you in improving your writing.

Then I asked ChatGPT to help create even more specific prompts and even asked for the first set of prompts to be regenerated. This is what I got on my second try:

My prompt: *How can I prompt you to improve my writing at the word, sentence, and discourse dimensions?*

ChatGPT's response: *To prompt me to improve your writing at the word, sentence, and discourse dimensions, you can follow these guidelines:*

1. *Word level improvements:*

   - **Request assistance with word choice:** *"Can you suggest more appropriate or precise words for this sentence?"*

   - **Seek help with vocabulary:** *"Are there any words in this paragraph that I could replace with more advanced or specific terms?"*

   - **Ask for clarification on word usage:** *"I'm unsure if I'm using this word correctly. Can you provide examples or explanations?"*

2. *Sentence level improvements:*

   - **Request feedback on sentence structure:** *"Could you review these sentences and suggest any modifications for better clarity or flow?"*

   - **Seek assistance with sentence variety:** *"How can I vary my sentence structure to make my writing more engaging?"*

   - **Ask for guidance on sentence transitions:** *"Can you suggest ways to improve the coherence and smoothness of my writing between sentences?"*

3. *Discourse level improvements:*

   - **Request feedback on paragraph organization:** *"Could you review the overall structure of my essay and suggest any improvements for better coherence?"*

   - **Seek guidance on logical flow:** *"How can I improve the transitions between paragraphs to ensure a smooth progression of ideas?"*

   - **Ask for assistance with maintaining focus and unity:** *"Do you have any suggestions for keeping my writing focused and ensuring that all ideas contribute to the main theme?"*

Remember, providing specific examples from your writing will help me give more targeted feedback. Feel free to ask for help at any of these dimensions or combine them in your request to address multiple aspects of your writing simultaneously.

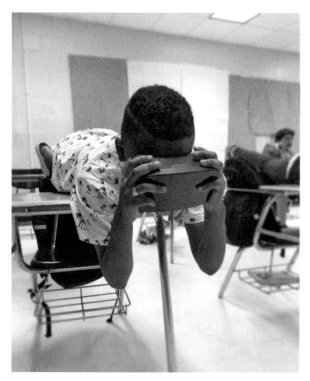

Figure 5–21 VR Can Take Students on Amazing Trips (Including Swimming in the Atlantic Ocean)

I was quite impressed by how on target these suggestions were. While there were no citations or references for these ideas, I can readily make those scholarly connections. If I had received responses that contradicted what I know to be effective pedagogy, I would rely on my own experience and disregard those responses. As always, digital tools are just that—*tools* to augment and not replace the teaching-learning process that happens through ongoing, authentic interactions among students and between students and their teachers. ELL teacher Victoria Seelinger creatively used virtual reality (VR) with her students, inviting them to choose and research a place anywhere in the world and then visit the place virtually. When a student chose Rio de Janeiro, he was able to share a wealth of information about Brazil. The class even took a virtual trip to the Christ the Redeemer statue and enjoyed a virtual swim at a nearby beach (see Figure 5–21).

Notice When Bridging Level Students Are Ready to Move On

Although most schools determine levels of language proficiency and student placement based on annual standardized assessments such as ACCESS by WIDA, ELPA21, and NYSESLAT, formative assessments and progress monitoring play an important role in your day-to-day work with MLs. To track the progress bridging level students are making, continue with a multidimensional approach. Your data collection should include teacher observations of oral language skills (listening and speaking), student work samples to document how their writing skills are developing, and reading conferences where you can check on their comprehension and also monitor how their reading skills are growing and to what degree they are able to use reading strategies.

You will start to notice that bridging level students are developing full capacity with the grade level target language skills when you can remove even more scaffolds or when their participation in all types of language and literacy learning activities approximates that of proficient English-speaking peers. For example, comparable to her English-proficient peers, Ruhi is likely to be able to read multiple texts on a target topic with minimal support, mainly focusing on contextual understanding and background building. Her writing will improve in length and complexity, revealing less frequent syntactic or semantic errors. And Delun will have prepared for his college education by engaging in more language-based explorations. He will expand his vocabulary and write and speak with more precision. Both students will take full advantage of digitally available resources to enhance their language and literacy development.

Works Cited

Adichie, Chimamanda Ngozi. 2009. "The Danger of a Single Story." Filmed July 2009 in Oxford, England. TED video, 18:33. https://www.ted.com/talks/chimamanda _ngozi_adichie_the_danger_of_a_single_story/c/transcript.

Almarode, John T., Douglas Fisher, and Nancy Frey. 2022. *How Feedback Works: A Playbook.* Thousand Oaks, CA: Corwin.

Anderson, Carl. 2018. *A Teacher's Guide to Writing Conferences: Classroom Essentials.* Portsmouth, NH: Heinemann.

Angelou, Maya. 2015. *I Know Why the Caged Bird Sings.* New York: Random House.

Asher, James J. 1981. "The Total Physical Response: Theory and Practice." *Annals of the New York Academy of Sciences* 379 (1): 324–31.

Auslander, Lisa. 2022. "Getting Newcomer English Learners off the Sidelines: Strategies for Increasing Learner Engagement While Developing Language and Literacy." *TESOL Journal* 00e1–6. https://doi.org/10.1002/tesj.647.

Ayer, Lauren. 2019. "All PBL Teachers Should Do These Things." TeachThought. March 15. https://www.teachthought.com/education/project-based-teachers/.

Bacak, Julie and Byker, Erik Jon. 2021. "Moving from Levels of Inquiry to the Flexible Phases of Inquiry Theory: A Literature Review of Inquiry-Based Teacher Education" *Journal of Teacher Education and Educators* 10 (2): 255–271.

Baker, Kyle. 2008. *Nat Turner.* New York: Abrams Comic Arts.

Baker, S., N. Lesaux, M. Jayanthi, J. Dimino, C. P. Proctor, J. Morris, R. Gersten, K. Haymond, M. J. Kieffer, S. Linan-Thompson, and R. Newman-Gonchar. 2014. *Teaching Academic Content and Literacy to English Learners in Elementary and Middle School.* NCEE 2014-4012. Washington, DC: National Center for Education Evaluation and Regional Assistance (NCEE), Institute of Education Sciences, U.S. Department of Education. https://ies.ed.gov/ncee/wwc/practiceguide/19.

Baldioli, Shannon. 2022. "The Case for Training Teachers in Object-Based Learning." *Smithsonian Education* (blog), June 7. https://www.smithsonianmag.com/blogs /smithsonian-education/2022/06/07/the-case-for-training-teachers-in-object -based-learning/.

Bambrick-Santoyo, Paul, Aja Settles, and Juliana Worrell. 2013. *Great Habits, Great Readers: A Practical Guide to K–4 Reading in Light of the Common Core.* San Francisco: Jossey-Bass.

Banchi, H., and R. Bell. 2008. "The Many Levels of Inquiry." *Science and Children* 46 (2): 26–29.

Beck, Isabel L., Margaret G. McKeown, and Linda Kucan. 2013. *Bringing Words to Life: Robust Vocabulary Instruction.* 2nd ed. New York: Guilford.

Billings, Elsa, and Aída Walqui. 2021. "Dispelling the Myth of 'English Only': Understanding the Importance of the First Language in Second Language Learning." New York State Education Department. Updated January 5. https://www.nysed.gov/bilingual-ed/topic-brief-5-dispelling-myth-english-only-understanding-importance-first-language.

Blaikie, Fiona. 2020. "Worlding Danny: Being, Becoming, and Belonging." *Studies in Art Education* 61 (4): 330–48. https://doi.org/10.1080/00393541.2020.1820831.

Buenrostro, Manuel, and Julie Maxwell-Jolly. 2021. *Renewing Our Promise: Research and Recommendations to Support California's Long-Term English Learners.* Long Beach, CA: Californians Together. https://californianstogether.org/wp-content/uploads/2021/10/Renewing_Our_Promise_to_LTELs.pdf.

Calderón, Margarita E., and Shawn Slakk. 2018. *Teaching Reading to English Learners, Grades 6–12: A Framework for Improving Achievement in the Content Areas.* Thousand Oaks, CA: Corwin.

Calhoun, Emily F. 1999. *Teaching Beginning Reading and Writing with the Picture Word Inductive Model.* Alexandria, VA: ASCD.

Capello, Marva, and Nancy T. Walker. 2016. "Visual Thinking Strategies: Teachers' Reflections on Closely Reading Complex Visual Texts Within the Disciplines." *Reading Teacher* 70 (3): 317–25. https://doi.org/10.1002/trtr.1523.

Carhill-Poza, Avary. 2019. "Defining Flipped Learning for English Learners in an Urban Secondary School." *Bilingual Research Journal* 42 (1): 90–104. https://doi.org/10.1080/15235882.2018.1561552.

CASEL. 2021. "Fundamentals of SEL." CASEL (website). https://casel.org/fundamentals-of-sel.

Christensen, Linda. 2010. "Putting Out the Linguistic Welcome Mat." *Wisconsin English Journal* 52 (1): 33–37.

Coe, Rob, C. J. Rauch, Stuart Kime, and Dan Singleton. 2020. *Great Teaching Toolkit: Evidence Review.* Sunderland, UK: Evidence Based Education. https://www.cambridgeinternational.org/Images/584543-great-teaching-toolkit-evidence-review.pdf.

Collins, Suzanne. 2008. *The Hunger Games.* New York: Scholastic.

Colorín Colorado. n.d. "'Welcome Kit' for New ELLs." Colorín Colorado (website). https://www.colorincolorado.org/article/welcome-kit-new-ells.

Cook, H. Gary, Tim Boals, Carsten Wilmes, and Martín Santos. 2008. "Issues in the Development of Annual Measurable Achievement Objectives for WIDA Consortium States." WCER Working Paper no. 2008-2. Madison, WI:

Wisconsin Center for Education Research. https://wcer.wisc.edu/docs/working -papers/Working_Paper_No_2008_02.pdf.

Cummins, Jim. 2005. "A Proposal for Action: Strategies for Recognizing Heritage Language Competence as a Learning Resource Within the Mainstream Classroom." *Modern Language Journal* 89 (4): 585–92.

Cummins, Sunday. 2017. "The Case for Multiple Texts." *Educational Leadership* 74 (5): 66–71.

Curiel, Lucía Cárdenas, and Christina M. Ponzio. 2021. "Imagining Multimodal and Translanguaging Possibilities for Authentic Cultural Writing Experiences." *Journal of Multilingual Education Research* 11: 79–102. https://doi.org/10.5422 /jmer.2021.v11.79-102.

Daniels, Jen, and Ruslana Westerlund. 2022. *Focus Bulletin: Scaffolding Learning for Multilingual Students in Math.* Madison, WI: Wisconsin Center for Education Research. https://wida.wisc.edu/sites/default/files/resource/FocusBulletin -Scaffolding-Learning-Multilingual-Students-Math.pdf.

de Jong, Esther J., Tuba Yilmaz, and Nidza Marichal. 2019. "Multilingualism-as-a -Resource Orientation in Dual Language Education." *Theory into Practice* 58 (2): 107–20.

de los Ríos, Cati V., and Kate Seltzer. 2017. "Translanguaging, Coloniality and English Classrooms: An Exploration of Two Bicoastal Urban Classrooms." *Research in the Teaching of English* 52 (1): 55–76.

de Oliveira, Luciana C. 2023. *Supporting Multilingual Learners' Academic Language Development.* New York: Routledge.

Dehaene, Stanislas. 2021. *How We Learn: Why Brains Learn Better Than Any Machine . . . for Now.* New York: Penguin Books.

Delpit, Lisa. 2013. *"Multiplications Is for White People": Raising Expectations for Other People's Children.* New York: The New Press.

Dodge, Judy, and Andrea Honigsfeld. 2014. *Core Instructional Routines: Go-to Structures for Literacy Learning in the K–5 Classroom.* Portsmouth, NH: Heinemann.

Dove, Maria G., and Andrea Honigsfeld. 2018. *Co-teaching for English Learners: A Guide to Collaborative Planning, Instruction, Assessment, and Reflection.* Thousand Oaks, CA: Corwin.

Dover, Alison J., and Fernando Rodríguez-Valls. 2022. *Radically Inclusive Teaching with Newcomer and Emergent Plurilingual Students.* New York: Teachers College Press.

Duke, Nell K., Samantha Caughlan, Mary M. Juzwik, and Nicole M. Martin. 2011. *Reading and Writing Genre with Purpose in K–8 Classrooms.* Portsmouth, NH: Heinemann.

Ehrenworth, Mary, Pablo Wolfe, and Marc Todd. 2021. *The Civically Engaged Classroom: Reading, Writing, and Speaking for Change.* Portsmouth, NH: Heinemann.

ELPA. 2016. *2016 ELPA21 Proficiency Descriptors.* Retrieved from https://www .oregon.gov/ode/educator-resources/assessment/Documents/elpa21 _proficiency_descriptors.pdf

España, Carla, and Luz Y. Herrera. 2020. *El communidad: Lessons for Centering the Voices and Experiences of Bilingual Latinx Students.* Portsmouth, NH: Heinemann.

Esteban-Guitart, Moisès, and Luis C. Moll. 2014. "Lived Experience, Funds of Identity and Education." *Culture and Psychology* 20 (1): 70–81.

Fairbairn, Shelley B., and Stephaney Jones-Vo. 2019. *Differentiating Instruction and Assessment for English Language Learners: A Guide for K–12 Teachers.* 2nd ed. Philadelphia: Caslon.

Fang, Zhihui. 2020. "Toward a Linguistically Informed, Responsive and Embedded Pedagogy in Secondary Literacy Instruction." *Journal of World Languages* 6 (1–2): 70–91. https://doi.org/10.1080/21698252.2020.1720161.

Fearn, Leif, and Nancy Farnan. 2001. *Interactions: Teaching Writing and the Language Arts.* Boston: Houghton Mifflin.

Ferlazzo, Larry, and Katie Hull Sypnieski. 2022. *The ESL/ELL Teacher's Survival Guide: Ready-to-Use Strategies, Tools, and Activities for Teaching All Levels.* 2nd ed. San Francisco: Jossey-Bass.

Fisher, Douglas, and Nancy Frey. 2014. *Checking for Understanding: Formative Assessment Techniques for Your Classroom.* 2nd ed. Alexandria, VA: ASCD.

Fisher, Douglas, Nancy Frey, and John Hattie. 2021. *The Distance Learning Playbook: Teaching for Engagement and Impact in Any Setting, Grades K–12.* Thousand Oaks, CA: Corwin.

Flipped Learning Network. 2014. "Definition of Flipped Learning." Flip Learning. March 12. https://flippedlearning.org/definition-of-Flipped-learning/.

French, Mei. 2018. "Multilingual Pedagogies in Practice." *TESOL in Context* 28 (1): 21–44.

Frey, Nancy, Douglas Fisher, and John Almarode. 2023. *How Scaffolding Works: A Playbook for Supporting and Releasing Responsibility to Students.* Thousand Oaks, CA: Corwin.

García, Ofelia. 2009. *Bilingual Education in the 21st Century: A Global Perspective.* Malden, MA: Wiley-Blackwell.

García, Ofelia, Susana Ibarra Johnson, and Kate Seltzer. 2017. *The Translanguaging Classroom: Leveraging Student Bilingualism for Learning.* Baltimore, MD: Brookes.

García, Ofelia, and Cristian R. Solorza. 2021. "Academic Language and the Minoritization of U.S. Bilingual Latinx Students." *Language and Education* 35 (6): 505–21.

Genesee, Fred. 2023. "The Home Language: An English Language Learner's Most Valuable Resource." Colorín Colorado. https://www.colorincolorado.org/article /home-language-english-language-learners-most-valuable-resource.

Gladwell, M. n.d. "Malcolm Gladwell Teaches Writing." MasterClass. https://www .masterclass.com/classes/malcolm-gladwell-teaches-writing.

Gonzalez, Valentina. 2020. "Rewriting the Narrative: ESL Teacher's Role." Rooted Linguistics LLC, Blog post 5/16/20. https://www.valentinaesl.com/blog /rewriting-the-narrative-esl-teachers-role.

———. 2022. "How to Use English Learners' Primary Language in the Classroom." Edutopia. December 13. https://www.edutopia.org/article/english-learners -primary-language-school/.

Goodwin, Bryan. 2020. *Learning That Sticks: A Brain-Based Model for K–12 Instructional Design and Delivery*. With Tonia Gibson and Kristin Rouleau. Alexandria, VA: ASCD.

Gottlieb, Margo. 2021. *Classroom Assessment in Multiple Languages: A Handbook for Teachers*. Thousand Oaks, CA: Corwin.

Gottlieb, Margo, and Gisela Ernst-Slavit. 2014. *Academic Language in Diverse Classrooms: Definitions and Contexts*. Thousand Oaks, CA: Corwin.

Greene, Jay P. November 2, 2016. Why do field trips matter? EdNext Podcast, Episode 59. Retrieved from http://educationnext.org/the-educational-value-of-field-trips/

Greene, Jay P., Collin Hitt, Anee Kraybill, and Cari A. Bogulski. 2015. "Learning from Live Theater: Students Realize Gains in Knowledge, Tolerance, and More." *Education Next* 15 (1): 54–61.

Greene, Jay P., Brian Kisida, and Daniel H. Bowen. 2014. "The Value of Field Trips." *Education Next* 14 (1): 78–86. https://app.education.nsw.gov.au/serap/ ResearchRecord/Summary?id=46.

Hattie, John, and Gregory C. R. Yates. 2014. *Visible Learning and the Science of How We Learn*. New York: Routledge.

Helman, Amanda, Minyi S. Dennis, and Lee Kern. 2022. "Clues: Using Generative Strategies to Improve the Science Vocabulary of Secondary English Learners with Reading Disabilities." *Learning Disability Quarterly* 45 (1): 19–31.

Helman, Lori, Carrie Rogers, Amy Frederick, and Maggie Struck. 2016. *Inclusive Literacy Teaching: Differentiating Approaches in Multilingual Elementary Classrooms*. New York: Teachers College Press.

Heritage, Margaret. 2022. *Formative Assessment: Making It Happen in the Classroom*. 2nd ed. Thousand Oaks, CA: Corwin.

Heritage, Margaret, Aída Walqui, and Robert Linquanti. 2015. *English Language Learners and the New Standards: Developing Language, Content Knowledge, and Analytical Practices in the Classroom.* Cambridge, MA: Harvard Education Press.

Heron, Marion, Sally Baker, Karen Gravett, and Evonne Irwin. 2023. "Scoping Academic Oracy in Higher Education: Knotting Together Forgotten Connections to Equity and Academic Literacies." *Higher Education Research and Development* 42 (1): 62–77. https://doi.org/10.1080/07294360.2022.2048635.

Hill, Jane D., and Kirsten B. Miller. 2014. *Classroom Instruction that Works with English Language Learners,* 2nd edition. Alexandria, VA: ASCD.

Hollie, Sharroky. 2017. *Culturally and Linguistically Responsive Teaching and Learning: Classroom Practices for Student Success, Grades K–12.* 2nd ed. Huntington Beach, CA: Shell Educational.

Honigsfeld, Andrea. 2019. *Growing Language and Literacy: Strategies for English Learners,* Grades K–8. Portsmouth, NH: Heinemann.

Honigsfeld, Andrea, and Maria G. Dove. 2021. *Co-Planning: Five Essential Practices to Integrate Curriculum and Instruction for English Learners.* Thousand Oaks, CA: Corwin.

Honigsfeld, Andrea, Maria G. Dove, Audrey Cohan, and Carrie McDermott Goldman. 2022. *From Equity Insights to Action: Critical Strategies for Teaching Multilingual Learners.* Thousand Oaks, CA: Corwin.

Honigsfeld, Andrea, and Jon Nordmeyer. 2023. "Stretching Your Co-teaching: Collaborating with WIDA." WIDA workshop, Rome, March 11–12, 2023.

Huynh, Tan, and Beth Skelton. 2023. *Long-Term Success for Experienced Multilinguals.* Thousand Oaks, CA: Corwin.

Khan, Minal. 2016. *Silk Tether.* New York: Yucca.

Khorram, Adib. 2019. *Darius the Great Is Not Okay.* New York: Dial Books.

Kim, YouJin, and Diane Belcher. 2020. "Multimodal Composing and Traditional Essays: Linguistic Performance and Learner Perceptions." *RELC Journal* 51 (1): 86–100. https://doi.org/10.1177/0033688220906943.

Krashen, Stephen D. 1988. *Second Language Acquisition and Second Language Learning.* New York: Prentice-Hall International.

Krashen, Stephen D., and Tracy D. Terrell. 1983. *The Natural Approach: Language Acquisition in the Classroom.* New York: Pergamon.

Ladson-Billings, Gloria. 2011. "But That's Just Good Teaching! The Case for Culturally Relevant Pedagogy." In *Thinking About Schools: A Foundations of Education Reader*, edited by Eleanor B. Hilty, 107–16. Boulder, CO: Westview.

Lahiri, Jhumpa. 2003. *The Namesake.* Boston: Mariner Books.

Lai, Thanhha. 2013. *Inside Out and Back Again.* New York: HarperCollins.

Lawrence, Michelle. n.d. "How to Support Social and Emotional Health of Middle/ High School ELLs." Colorín Colorado. https://www.colorincolorado.org/article /social-and-emotional-needs-middle-and-high-school-ells.

Learning Policy Institute and Turnaround for Children. 2021. *Design Principles for Schools: Putting the Science of Learning and Development into Action.* Palo Alto, CA, and Tempe, AZ: Authors. https://k12.designprinciples.org/sites/default /files/SoLD_Design_Principles_REPORT.pdf.

Lee, Andrew M. I. n.d. "What Is Self-Advocacy?" Understood. https://www.understood .org/en/articles/the-importance-of-self-advocacy.

Lee, Harper. 2018. *To Kill a Mockingbird: A Graphic Novel.* Adapted and illustrated by Fred Fordham. New York: HarperCollins.

Lenters, Kimberly. 2016. "Telling 'a Story of Somebody' Through Digital Scrapbooking: A Fourth Grade Multi-Literacies Project Takes an Affective Turn." *Literacy Research and Instruction* 55 (3): 262–83. http://dx.doi.org/10.1080/19388071 .2016.1162234.

Leon, Jennifer. 2020. *Don't Ask Me Where I Am From.* New York: Simon and Schuster.

Lyman, Frank. 1981. "The Responsive Classroom Discussion: The Inclusion of All Students." In *Mainstreaming Digest: A Collection of Faculty and Student Papers,* edited by Audrey Springs Anderson, 109–13. College Park, MD: University of Maryland.

Marshall, Helaine W. 2019. "6 Models of Flipped Learning Instruction." *TESOL Connections,* April. http://newsmanager.commpartners.com/tesolc/issues/2019 -04-01/2.html.

Martínez-Álvarez, Patricia. 2017. "Special Ways of Knowing in Science: Expansive Learning Opportunities with Bilingual Children with Learning Disabilities." *Cultural Studies of Science Education* 12 (3): 521–53. https://doi.org/10.1007 /s11422-016-9732-x.

Massaro, Dominic W. 2017. "Reading Aloud to Children: Benefits and Implications for Acquiring Literacy Before Schooling Begins." *The American Journal of Psychology* 130 (1): 63–72.

McInerney, Kristen. 2023. "Perceptions from Newcomer Multilingual Adolescents: Predictors and Experiences of Sense of Belonging in High School." *Child and Youth Care Forum* 52: 1041–72. https://doi.org/10.1007/s10566-022-09723-8.

Medina, Jane. 1999. *My Name Is Jorge: On Both Sides of the River.* Honesdale, PA: Wordsong.

Miller, Debbie. 2013. *Reading with Meaning: Teaching Comprehension in the Primary Grades.* 2nd ed. Portland, ME: Stenhouse.

Miller, Donalyn, and Teri Lesesne. 2022. *The Joy of Reading.* Portsmouth: Heinemann.

Minkel, Justin. 2018. "Being an English-Language Learner Is Hard: Here Are 5 Ways Teachers Can Make It Easier." *Education Week*, February 7. https://www.edweek.org/tm/articles/2018/02/07/being-an-english-language-learner-is-hard-here.html.

Moeller, Babette. 2022. "Encouraging Student Self-Advocacy in the Mathematics Classroom." *Math for All* (blog), March 28. https://mathforall.edc.org/encouraging-student-self-advocacy-in-the-mathematics-classroom/.

Moll, Luis C., Cathy Amanti, Deborah Neff, and Norma Gonzalez. 1992. "Funds of Knowledge for Teaching: Using a Qualitative Approach to Connect Homes and Classrooms." *Theory into Practice* 31 (2): 132–41.

Moore, Kristi. 2021. "How to Bring Guided Reading to High School English." *Moore English* (blog). https://moore-english.com/how-to-bring-guided-reading-to-high-school-english/.

Morrison, Judith, Yuliya Ardasheva, Sarah Newcomer, Lindsay Lightner, Gisela Ernst-Slavit, and Kira Carbonneau. 2020. "Supporting Science Learning for English Language Learners." *Journal of Educational Research and Practice* 10 (1): 254–74.

Muhammad, Gholdy. 2020. *Cultivating Genius: An Equity Framework for Culturally and Historically Responsive Literacy.* New York: Scholastic.

———. 2023. *Unearthing Joy: A Guide to Culturally and Historically Responsive Teaching and Learning.* New York: Scholastic.

National Education Association. 2015. *How Educators Can Advocate for English Language Learners (ELLs): All In!* Washington, DC: Author. https://www.colorincolorado.org/sites/default/files/ELL_AdvocacyGuide2015.pdf.

Noonoo, Stephen. 2023. "Using Infographics to Build Media Literacy and Higher-Order Thinking Skills." Edutopia. January 20. https://www.edutopia.org/article/infographics-media-literacy-skills/.

Nordmeyer, Jon, Tim Boals, Rita MacDonald, and Ruslana Westerlund. 2021. "What Does Equity Really Mean for Multilingual Learners?" *Educational Leadership* 78 (6): 60–65.

Nyachae, Tiffany M. 2019. "Social Justice Literacy Workshop for Critical Dialogue." *Journal of Adolescent and Adult Literacy* 63 (1): 106–10.

OECD. 2018. *The Resilience of Students with an Immigrant Background: Factors That Shape Well-Being.* Paris: Author. http://dx.doi.org/10.1787/9789264292093-en.

Ohta, Amy S. 2001. *Second Language Acquisition Processes in the Classroom: Learning Japanese.* Mahwah, NJ: Lawrence Erlbaum.

Ottow, Sarah B. 2023. *The Language Lens for Content Classrooms: A Guidebook for Teachers, Coaches and Leaders.* 2nd ed. Cumberland, RI: Confianza.

Oxford, Rebecca. 2017. *Teaching and Researching Language Learning Strategies: Self-Regulation in Context.* 2nd ed. New York: Routledge.

Pacheco, Mark B., Shannon M. Daniel, and Lisa C. Pray. 2017. "Scaffolding Practice: Supporting Emerging Bilinguals' Academic Language Use in Two Classroom Communities." *Language Arts* 95 (2): 63–76.

Pacheco, Mark B., Shannon M. Daniel, Lisa C. Pray, and Robert T. Jiménez. 2019. "Translingual Practice, Strategic Participation, and Meaning-Making." *Journal of Literacy Research* 51 (1): 75–99. https://journals.sagepub.com/doi/10.1177/1086296X18820642.

Pahl, Kate, and Steve Pool. 2020. "Hoping: The Literacies of the 'Not Yet.'" In *Living Literacies: Literacy for Social Change*, by Kate Pahl and Jennifer Rowsell, with Diane Collier, Steve Pool, Zanib Rasool, and Terry Trzecak, 67–90. Cambridge, MA: MIT Press.

Paraiso, Johanna. 2022. "Using Technology to Boost Confidence." Teaching Channel video, 2:44 min. https://learn.teachingchannel.com/video/technology-to-help-students-ousd.

Paris, Django. 2012. "Culturally Sustaining Pedagogy: A Needed Change in Stance, Terminology, and Practice." *Educational Researcher* 41 (3): 93–97.

Parker, Kimberly N. 2022. *Literacy Is Liberation: Working Toward Justice Through Culturally Relevant Teaching.* Alexandria, VA: ASCD.

Parker, Walter C. 2006. "Public Discourses in Schools: Purposes, Problems, Possibilities." *Educational Researcher* 35 (8): 11–18.

Parrish, N. 2022. "Teaching Students to Assess Their Learning." Edutopia. May 23. https://www.edutopia.org/article/teaching-students-assess-their-learning.

Pierce, Brett. 2022. *Expanding Literacy: Bringing Digital Storytelling into Your Classroom.* Portsmouth, NH: Heinemann.

Ramirez, Pablo, and Lydia Ross. 2019. "Secondary Dual-Language Learners and Emerging Pedagogies: The Intersectionality of Language, Culture, and Community." *Theory into Practice* 58 (2): 176–84. https://doi.org/10.1080/00405841.2019.1569399.

Rhodes, Catherine R., Katherine Clonan-Roy, and Stanton E. F. Wortham. 2021. "Making Language 'Academic': Language Ideologies, Enregisterment, and Ontogenesis." *Language and Education* 35 (6): 522–38. https://www.tandfonline.com/doi/full/10.1080/09500782.2020.1797771.

Ritchhart, Ron, and Mark Church. 2020. *The Power of Making Thinking Visible: Practices to Engage and Empower All Learners.* San Francisco: Jossey-Bass.

Robertson, Kristina. n.d. "Increase Student Interaction with 'Think-Pair-Shares' and 'Circle Chats.'" Colorín Colorado. https://www.colorincolorado.org/article/increase-student-interaction-think-pair-shares-and-circle-chats.

Rubin, Heather, Lisa Estrada, and Andrea Honigsfeld. 2022. *Digital-Age Teaching for English Learners: A Guide to Equitable Learning for All Students.* 2nd ed. Thousand Oaks, CA: Corwin.

Russell, Karen. 2007. *St. Lucy's Home for Girls Raised by Wolves.* New York: Vintage.

Sahakyan, Narek. 2013. *District-Level Analysis of ELL Growth.* Madison, WI: Wisconsin Center for Education Research. https://wida.wisc.edu/sites/default/files/resource/Report-DistrictLevelAnalysisOfELLGrowth.pdf.

Salva, Carol. 2017. *Boosting Achievement: Reaching Students with Interrupted or Minimal Education.* With Anna Matis. San Clemente, CA: Seidlitz Education.

Samway, Katharine D., Lucinda Pease-Alvarez, and Laura Alvarez. 2020. *Supporting Newcomer Students: Advocacy and Instruction for English Learners.* New York: W. W. Norton.

Saunders, William G., and Gisela O'Brien. 2006. "Oral Language." In *Educating English Language Learners: A Synthesis of Research Evidence*, edited by Fred Genesee, Kathryn Lindholm-Leary, William Saunders, and Donna Christian, 14–48. New York: Cambridge University Press.

Schwartz, Laurel. 2020. "Teaching Target Language Vocabulary with Micro Field Trips." Edutopia. May 26. https://www.edutopia.org/article/teaching-target-language-vocabulary-micro-field-trips/.

Seidlitz, John, and Bill Perryman. 2021. *7 Steps to a Language-Rich, Interactive Classroom.* Second ed. Irving, TX: Seidlitz Education.

Shafer Willner, L., M. Gottlieb, F. M. Kray, R. Westerlund, C. Lundgren, S. Besser, E. Warren, A. Cammilleri, and M. E. Cranley. 2020. "Appendix F: Theoretical Foundations of the WIDA English Language Development Standards Framework, 2020 Edition." In *WIDA English Language Development Standards Framework, 2020 Edition: Kindergarten–Grade 12*, by WIDA, 354–74. Madison, WI: Board of Regents of the University of Wisconsin System. https://wida.wisc.edu/sites/default/files/resource/WIDA-ELD-Standards-Framework-2020.pdf.

Shanahan, Cynthia, and Timothy Shanahan. 2020. "Disciplinary Literacy." In *The SAT Suite and Classroom Practice: English Language Arts/Literacy*, edited by Jim Patterson, 91–125. New York: College Board.

Shanahan, Timothy. 2018. "What Do You Think About Guided Reading for Secondary School?" *Shanahan on Literacy* (blog), October 2. https://www.readingrockets.org/blogs/shanahan-literacy/what-do-you-think-guided-reading-secondary-school.

Singer, Tonya Ward, and Diane Staehr Fenner. 2020. "From Watering Down to Challenging." In *Breaking Down the Wall: Essential Shifts for English Learners' Success*, by Margarita Espino Calderón, Maria G. Dove, Diane Staehr Fenner, Margo Gottlieb, Andrea Honigsfeld, Tonya Ward Singer, Shawn Slakk, Ivannia Soto, and Debbie Zacarian, 47–71. Thousand Oaks, CA: Corwin.

Smith, Jennifer M., and Marla K. Robertson. 2021. "(Info)Graphically Inclined: A Framework of Infographic Learning." *The Reading Teacher* 74 (4): 439–49. https://doi.org/10.1002/trtr.1966.

Snyder, Sydney, and Diane Staehr Fenner. 2021. *Culturally Responsive Teaching for Multilingual Learners: Tools for Equity.* Thousand Oaks, CA: Corwin.

Soto, Ivannia. 2014. *Moving from Spoken to Written Language with ELLs.* Thousand Oaks, CA: Corwin.

Spencer, John. 2022. "Designing Socratic Seminars to Ensure That All Students Can Participate." John Spencer (website). September 24. https://spencerauthor.com/socratic-seminars/.

Spencer, John and A.J. Juliani. 2017. *Empower: What Happens When Students Own Their Learning.* IMPress, LP.

Spies, Tracy G., and Yunying Xu. 2018. "Scaffolded Academic Conversations: Access to 21st-Century Collaboration and Communication Skills." *Intervention in School and Clinic* 54 (1): 22–30.

Stewart, Mandy A., Holly Hansen-Thomas, Patricia Flint, and Mariannella Núñez. 2021. "Translingual Disciplinary Literacies: Equitable Language Environments to Support Literacy Engagement." *Reading Research Quarterly* 57 (1): 181–203. https://doi:10.1002/rrq.381.

Stiggins, Richard J., Judith A. Arter, Jan Chappuis, and Stephen Chappuis. 2020. *Classroom Assessment for Student Learning: Doing It Right—Using It Well.* 3rd edition. Hoboken, NJ: Pearson Education.

Surma, Tim, Gino Camp, Renate de Groot, and Paul A. Kirschner. 2022. "Novice Teachers' Knowledge of Effective Study Strategies." *Frontiers in Education* 7. https://www.frontiersin.org/articles/10.3389/feduc.2022.996039/full.

Symons, Carrie, and Yue Bian. 2022. "Exploring a Linguistic Orientation to Facilitating Refugee-Background Youth's Meaning-Making with Texts: A Self-Study." *Linguistics and Education* 70: 101031. https://doi.org/10.1016/j.linged.2022.101031.

Thompson, Laurie Ann. 2015. *Emmanuel's Dream: The True Story of Emmanuel Ofosu Yeboah.* Toronto, ON: Anne Schwartz Books.

Thorpe, Helen. 2017. *The Newcomers: Finding Refuge, Friendship, and Hope in an American Classroom.* New York: Scribner.

Trelease, Jim. 2019. *Jim Trelease's Read-Aloud Handbook.* 8th ed. Edited and revised by Cyndi Girogis. New York: Penguin.

Tung, Rosann. 2013. "Innovations in Educational Equity for English Language Learners." Special issue: English Language Learners: Shifting to an Asset-Based Paradigm. *Voices in Urban Education* 37: 2–5. https://files.eric.ed.gov/fulltext/EJ1046319.pdf.

Umansky, Ilana, Megan Hopkins, Dafney B. Dabach, Lorna Porter, Karen Thompson, and Delia Pompa. 2018. *Understanding and Supporting the Educational Needs of Recently Arrived Immigrant English Learner Students: Lessons for State and Local Education Agencies.* Washington, DC: Council of Chief State School Officers.

Valdés, Guadalupe, Luis Poza, and Maneka Deanna Brooks. 2017. "Language Acquisition in Bilingual Education." In *The Handbook of Bilingual and Multilingual Education*, edited by Wayne E. Wright, Sovicheth Boun, and Ofelia García, 56–74. Malden, MA: Wiley-Blackwell.

Van Der Wende, Carly. 2021. "Using Read-Aloud to Boost Students' Creativity." Edutopia. December 17. https://www.edutopia.org/article/using-read-alouds-boost-students-creativity.

Velasco, Patricia, and Ofelia García. 2014. "Translanguaging and the Writing of Bilingual Learners." *Bilingual Research Journal* 37 (1): 6–23.

Vu, Don. 2021. *Life, Literacy and the Pursuit of Happiness: Supporting Our Immigrant and Refugee Children Through the Power of Reading.* New York: Scholastic.

Vygotsky, Lev. 1978. *Mind in Society: The Development of Higher Psychological Processes.* Cambridge: Cambridge University Press.

Walqui, Aída. 2006. "Scaffolding Instruction for English Language Learners: A Conceptual Framework." *International Journal of Bilingual Education and Bilingualism* 9 (2): 159–80.

Washor, Elliot, and Charles Mojkowski. 2013. *Leaving to Learn: How Out-of-School Learning Increases Student Engagement and Reduces Dropout Rates.* Portsmouth, NH: Heinemann.

Weinstein, Daniel. 2021. "Terrific Techniques from the Past Two Years." *The Creativity Core* (blog), July 26. https://www.thecreativitycore.com/the-blog.

Weinstein, Yana, Christopher R. Madan, and Megan A. Sumeracki. 2018. "Teaching the Science of Learning." *Cognitive Research* 3 (1): 2. https://doi.org/10.1186/s41235-017-0087-y.

WIDA. 2020. *WIDA English Language Development Standards Framework, 2020 Edition: Kindergarten–Grade 12.* Madison, WI: Board of Regents of the University of Wisconsin System. https://wida.wisc.edu/sites/default/files/resource/WIDA-ELD-Standards-Framework-2020.pdf.

———. 2021. *FAQ Series: Key Language Uses.* Madison, WI: Board of Regents of the University of Wisconsin System. https://wida.wisc.edu/sites/default/files/Website/News/2021/February/WIDA-StandardsFAQ-%20KeyLanguageUses.pdf.

Yenawine, Philip. 2013. *Visual Thinking Strategies: Using Art to Deepen Learning Across School Disciplines.* Cambridge, MA: Harvard Education Press.

Zwiers, Jeff. 2014. *Building Academic Language: Meeting Common Core Standards Across Disciplines, Grades 5–12.* 2nd ed. San Francisco: Jossey-Bass.

———. 2019a. *The Communication Effect: How to Enhance Learning by Building Ideas and Bridging Information Gaps.* Thousand Oaks, CA: Corwin.

———. 2019b. *Next Steps with Academic Conversations: New Ideas for Improving Learning Through Classroom Talk.* Grandview Heights, OH: Stenhouse.